REACHING SENIOR
LEADERSHIP

10 Growth Strategies Every Government Leader Should Know

EDITED BY ALEX D. TREMBLE
The Federal Career Coach

REVIEWS

"Looking for your personal success story in the federal government? 'Reaching Senior Leadership: 10 Growth Strategies Every Government Leader Should Know' is an excellent go-to for anyone wanting to excel as a government employee. Using his own career and experiences as examples, Alex Tremble provides unique insights into the varied workings of federal employment, offering solid examples, coupled with a practical approach to success."

Gail A. Adams

- Former Director of Intergovernmental & External Affairs, U.S. Department of the Interior (Former Senior Executive Service)
- Current Vice President of Communications & External Affairs, International Association of Geophysical Contractors

---

"From the first page to the last, the material immediately captures your attention and continues to provide information on strategizing your professional career growth. This book will provide the reader with ideas and strategies to grow their careers and provides techniques on how best to work with senior management by interacting and growing your career in different environments. I wish I had this book when I began my Federal career over 32 years ago. I highly recommend readers to use this book as a reference in their tool box and revisit the materials over and over again."

Fredericka Joseph

- Retired Senior Federal Leader
- Current Chair, Society of American Indian Government Employees Board of Directors

---

"Alex Tremble is a young man with a tremendous amount of intellectual curiosity and a zeal for helping others. This book is one indication of just that. I am particularly moved by "The Cost of Reaching Your Goals" section and inspired by Ms. Martin's journey from GS-2 to SES. I am humbled and excited to be one of Alex's many mentors."

Joe Ward

- Former Director, U.S. Department of the Interior, National Business Center (Retired Senior Executive Service)
- Current Director, Federal Shared Services, KPMG US

TABLE OF CONTENTS

INTRODUCTION

Years ago, shortly after securing my first position with the Federal Government, I had lunch with a young human resources specialist. We discussed our career aspirations and speculated on the impact of the then pending Federal Government retirement wave on our fledgling careers. Even at that young stage in our careers, we recognized that the retirement wave would create opportunities for skilled leaders ready to replace the high number of senior leaders that would be retiring. We concluded that if we secured the right training and experience and developed the right networks, in combination with patience and hard work, we would position ourselves for senior-level positions when the wave hit. I am happy to share that our plan worked perfectly.

Those who would argue that we were in the right place at the right time are partially right. As Malcolm Gladwell explained in his bestselling book *Outliers*, our environment plays a significant role in how successful we become or fail to become. There is, indeed, a perfect time to be born that will allow you to take advantage of particular opportunities. If you want to become a senior leader in the Federal Government, the perfect time to have been born was approximately 25 to 35 years ago so that you were ready to take advantage of the opportunities coming within the next 5 years.

As of the publishing of this book, the Federal Government is on the brink of a transformation unlike anything it has seen in decades. Nearly 3 in 10 U.S. Government employees will be eligible for retirement in 2023 (Katz, 2018). We just completed the longest partial Government shutdown in the history of the United States, and swarms of employees are retiring or leaving the Federal Government for the nongovernmental sector (Wagner, 2018). Many of the remaining employees fear the "brain drain" taking place and/or feel frustrated because many of the positions being vacated are not being refilled, resulting in increased responsibility for those who remain. So, what does all this mean for you?

If you are prepared, from a sheer numbers perspective, the Federal sector is in the early stages of an opportunity explosion.

The significant number of Federal employees exiting the Government, coupled with the fact that many of those positions are not being backfilled, means that there is a mounting need for senior-level leaders. And, given that the Government's workload has almost never decreased, it is only a matter of time before the Government begins an inevitable hiring campaign. Thus, those who are strategically prepared for this mass hiring will be best positioned to attain the most senior level positions within the Government. As I explain to my Federal and private-sector clients, those dedicated to strategically positioning themselves now will reap the benefits tomorrow.

How This Book Is Structured

The path to reaching our goals can be easily summed up in what I call my GPS Success Model. The "G" stands for a clearly defined *goal* so we know where we are going, the "P" stands for a strategic *plan* so we know which tactics to use to get there, and the "S" stands for *stamina* (e.g., resilience) so that we have the energy and motivation to keep going. This book is primarily focused on sharing tactics that you can employ to help you reach your goals. In addition to this book, I encourage you to read *The GPS Guide to Success* to learn more about goal setting and the model as a whole.

To help you on your journey to career success, this book discusses 10 key areas of growth:

- Leveraging your strengths
- Recognizing leadership myths
- Engaging in collective problem solving
- Achieving success as a younger leader
- Developing executive presence
- Understanding and working with political appointees
- Building relationships
- Perfecting your Federal resume

- Recognizing the cost of reaching your goals
- Overcoming discrimination

I provide a short introduction at the beginning of each chapter before introducing one of my colleagues for a deeper dive into the topic. Each section has been designed to provide you with practical steps you can take today to begin positioning yourself for your next promotion.

Without further ado, it is time to begin your career and growth journey.

References

Katz, E. (2018, June 18). The Federal Agencies where the most employees are eligible to retire. *Government Executive.* Retrieved from https://www.govexec.com/pay-benefits/2018/06/federal-agencies-where-most-employees-are-eligible-retire/149091/

Wagner, E. (2018, August 6). Federal retirement claims up nearly 16 percent so far in 2018 over the same period last year. *Government Executive.* Retrieved from

https://www.govexec.com/pay-benefits/2018/08/federal-retirement-claims-nearly-16-percent-so-far-2018-over-same-period-last-year/150310/

LEVERAGING OUR STRENGTHS

Weﾠnow live in arguably the most complex world that has ever existed. Due to international commerce, technology, and easily accessible information, the world has gotten smaller and the ability to successfully climb the leadership ladder as an average employee has all but vanished. As stated by internationally acclaimed author, entrepreneur, philanthropist, and life coach Tony Robbins, "People don't buy average anymore." He is right. With so much competition in the world, why would hiring managers settle for average? The quickest way to become an expert is by investing our time, energy, and resources into further developing the skills we are already good at. If you devote 50% more energy towards improving something you are already good at, you can become great! But if you devote 50% more energy towards improving something you are bad at, you can only become average.

Thus, Federal employees hoping to stand out and rise to the Government's most senior levels must focus on developing their strengths. Just as important as becoming an expert, if not more important, is being perceived as an expert. It does not help you or your career to be the best-kept secret. I mean, wouldn't you want to walk into a room and instantly be recognized as a thought leader who should be listened to? My coaching clients and group mentoring participants are always surprised at how much they can influence the perceptions of others using the strategies I teach them.

For a deeper dive into the importance of leveraging your strengths, I reached out to expert leadership development coach Monique Betty. In addition to being a Certified Executive Coach, Gallup Certified Strengths Coach, and President of CareerSYNC, Coach Monique is a nationally recognized leadership development expert dedicated to the advancement of diverse professionals in the workplace.

Leading a Strengths-Based Career

by Monique 'Coach Monique' Betty

I believe in the premise that every ambitious professional can build a stronger career by becoming a strength-based leader. And how do you do that? It begins with self-awareness by *knowing* your talents, then *applying* your talents in the workplace and then *creating lasting impact* with your talents.

When considering what it means for you to become a strength-based leader, how does the idea *of waking up every day and doing what you do best* sound to you?

When Gallup revealed its findings from a 40-year study of human strengths, the strengths-based movement began. It is now a global phenomenon, as the CliftonStrengths assessment has been translated into more than 20 languages.

3x

Report having excellent
quality of life

Millions of people were surveyed on the topic of employee engagement, and only one-third of respondents strongly agreed with the statement: *"At work I have the opportunity to do what I do best every day."*

Emerging from the Gallup findings is that people were engaged at work for reasons beyond pay, benefits, senior management, or organizational structure. When people have the opportunity to focus on their strengths every day, they are six times more likely to be engaged in their jobs and more than *three times* more likely to report having an excellent quality of life in general (Flade, Asplund, & Elliot, 2015).

In 1999, I was first introduced to the CliftonStrengths research and insights while attending a Coca-Cola Company senior leadership meeting in Las Vegas, Nevada. The keynote speaker was Marcus Buckingham, author of *First, Break All the Rules.* It was a 'drop the mic' moment for me when I heard him say that the research supports the notion of *strength-building* as the way forward in professional development versus *weakness-fixing,* which is the conventional approach. That was all it took for me to join the movement. Hardwired with positivity (yes, *positivity* is in fact my #1 signature theme!), I am a firm believer that the glass is half-full and in developing people from their natural place of strengths rather than trying to fix something that is a deficit.

The Office of Personnel Management's September 2015 report, *Engaging the Federal Workforce: How to Do It & Prove It,* defines employee engagement as "the employee's sense of purpose that is evident in their display of dedication, persistence, and effort in their work or overall attachment to their organization and its mission" (p. 1).

In terms of professional development, the traditional approach of *weakness-fixing* was built on the following principles:

- Most behaviors can be learned.
- The best in a role display the same behaviors.
- Weakness fixing leads to success.

In comparison, professional development for the *strengths-building* approach adheres to these principles:

- Only some behaviors can be learned.
- The best in a role deliver the same outcomes using different behaviors.
- Weakness fixing prevents failure, while strength building leads to success.

"What lies behind us, and what lies in front of us, are tiny matters compared to what lies within us."
—Henry David Thoreau

Focusing first on *you*, there is value in *knowing* your strengths. Armed with this information, you begin the journey of awareness and understanding of what propels your thoughts, feelings, and beliefs. Going forward with this knowledge, you are now equipped to *apply* your strengths in such a way that you take action and perform in a way that builds confidence, focus, and hope, as you are in control of driving your career.

To understand a strength is to understand its composition. A strength is composed of a collection of *natural talents* that are within you. When these talents (natural ways of thinking, feeling, or behaving) are nurtured and developed through investments in practice, skills, and knowledge, they evolve to a strength, which is the ability to consistently produce a specific positive outcome. For the ambitious professional, positive outcomes are the fuel for career advancement.

Gallup findings uncovered that people working in their strengths zone:

- Look forward to going into work
- Have more positive than negative interactions with coworkers
- Treat customers better

Knowing Your Strengths

As an ambitious professional, consider how your talents contribute to your work performance as a Federal employee.

- How do you evaluate your relationships with your boss, administrators, colleagues, and others?
- How do you evaluate your daily behaviors, actions, and overall professional style? Are you open, engaging, and interesting? Or are you defensive, opinionated, and self-absorbed?

Your answers to questions like these help you gain self-awareness, which is an important element in effectively managing your job performance and ultimately your career.

The challenge for most people is finding the way to describe their workplace relationships and behaviors in a meaningful way that informs them of how to make specific performance improvements. This is how the CliftonStrengths assessment serves as a valuable resource.

Here are the steps toward discovering your natural talents and ultimately your strengths:

- Complete the online CliftonStrengths assessment. (Purchase either the **CS Top 5,** which is a brief report of your most dominant talents, or **CS 34,** which is the expanded report of all of your talents in rank order.)
- Review your personalized **Strengths Insights Report.**
- Create an action plan for using your strengths toward accomplishing your workplace goals.

By discovering your talents and strengths, you gain

- Increased self-awareness, the capacity to recognize when you do what you do and why you do it
- Increased self-expression, how you show up and express yourself
- Increased self-regulation, the emotional well-being representative of your behavior and having the ability to act in a manner that is best for the team and the organization

Applying Your Strengths

Since 2010, I have conducted team workshops and coached individuals in developing strategic plans for achieving peak performance at work. A valuable aspect of the planning work is the rich insight gained through the awareness of team and individual strengths.

The following **Strengths in Action** provide examples of how Federal employees applied their personalized strengths insights.

Table 1: Denise the Congressional Staffer.

	Signature theme	Challenge	Action steps	Outcome
Denise, professional staff member for U.S. congressman	**Responsibility**: Takes psychological ownership of what she says she will do. Committed to stable values such as honesty and loyalty.	Has a hard time creating boundaries at work and takes on too much work, which has left her feeling burnt out.	Share the ownership of projects. Push yourself to say no. Partner with someone who will help you stay on track and prevent overload.	Reduced stress. Had more time for activities outside of work.

Note: Your "Signature theme" is identified by taking the CliftonStrengths assessment.

I clearly remember the moment when Denise became aware of her dominant Responsibility theme. Her eyes flew open, she sat back in her chair, and she said, "This is why I am so burnt out! I take work personally and I don't know how to tell someone 'no'!"

The clarity was powerful. Armed with this clarity, she took steps to change her situation.

Table 2. Karen From Homeland Security.

	Signature theme	Challenge	Action steps	Outcome
Karen, Homeland Security and Federal Emergency Management Agency	**Context**: Enjoys thinking about the past. Understands the present by researching its history.	As a 15-year employee, she was tasked with completing an *efficiency study* to cut costs and/or reduce turnaround time on projects. As with others dominant in Context, she found embracing new ideas challenging because she focused on what did or did not work in past experiences.	Verify her tendency to draw on the past in many dimensions of her life. Give herself time boundaries for sorting through the past for relevant information. Partner with her boss to hold herself accountable.	Decreased the time for completing the efficiency study.

When Karen's Context theme was identified and understood by all members of her team, relationships became collaborative rather than combative. Several of Karen's coworkers interpreted her many references to the past as an attempt to derail the efficiency study because she frequently argued for why something was not going to be successful. In fact, Karen thought that her references to the past were helping the team understand as they were considering present-day actions.

So, going forward, as you consider how your strengths will be applied to success in your job, consider what you know to be true about yourself in an effort to promote successful partnerships.

Table 3. Bryan From the Department of Defense.

	Signature theme	Challenge	Action steps	Outcome
Bryan: Procurement analyst, Department of Defense	**Learner**: Has a great desire to learn and continuously improve. Views the process of learning as exciting.	By asking so many questions, he caused his supervisor to think that he was using stall tactics in order to conduct endless research.	Gain agreement with his supervisor to think through his questions first and then present her with only the most important.	Improved relationship with supervisor.

During a workshop I conducted, with a seven-person group in Washington, DC, Bryan was so proud to understand his dominant Learner theme. He shared with the group his broad and deep curiosity to learn, particularly about human behavior. He was always the one who caused meetings to run beyond their scheduled time because he had question after question.

Soon his supervisor came to realize that this was why he asked so many questions when given a task. As she had the dominant theme of Achiever, which is hardwired for getting things done, she was often frustrated with his constant questioning and started to view him as having ineffective time management and prioritization skills.

As she realized that Bryan's Learner theme was behind his constant cycle of questions, the two were able to develop a plan. When given a new assignment, Bryan agreed to review the required work and write down his three most pressing questions related to the task at hand. This encouraged him to be precise with his questions, and she found her inner patience.

Relationships at Work

When considering engagement at work, relationships are key. An essential element of relationships is the ability for collaboration. An interesting insight in Gallup's research is the response to this question, "How many strong alliances do you have at work?" The most common answer: zero.

The best predictor of employee engagement is whether or not the employee likes the people she or he is working with at that moment. People who have a best friend at work are *seven times* more likely to be engaged in their jobs.

When the talents of all team members are revealed and understood, there is the opportunity for gaining clarity on what contributions everyone can bring to the table.

There are three fundamental perspectives for creating successful workplace partnerships (Wagner & Muller, 2019).

1. We complement each other's strengths.
2. We need each other to get the job done.
3. My teammate does some things much better than I do, and I do some things much better than my teammate does.

Gaining meaningful awareness of the talents of colleagues supports a cooperative workplace and, as a result, supports employee engagement.

Create Lasting Impressions in Your Career

I am often asked, "How do I use this information to inform me of my career choices?" Because CliftonStrengths is not a career inventory instrument, it does not suggest career paths. However, by knowing your talents, you can develop them in whatever roles you are in throughout your life. In time, you will discover which environments allow you to bring out your best.

As with other key elements of self-awareness, such as character traits, values, motivations, and life purpose, knowing your talents is one view of the mosaic known as *you*. With increased self-awareness comes increased career and life self-management.

I often encourage ambitious professionals to discuss strengths during performance reviews. If your current job doesn't offer opportunities to leverage your talents, ask your supervisor to be on the lookout for special assignments or projects that allow you to put your talents to work.

An interesting element in understanding your CliftonStrengths is that your dominant talents are not operating alone; in other words, they are illuminated to varying degrees when combined with your other dominant talents. Two examples are provided below.

Table 4. Example CliftonStrengths Themes.

Example	Theme 1	Theme 2	Combined themes
1	**Ideation,** *fascinated by ideas. Finds connections between seemingly random things.*	**Relator,** *enjoys close relationships with others.*	While being socially selective and preferring to deepen existing relationship, my mind is open and willing to create new experiences.
2	**Ideation,** *fascinated by ideas. Finds connections between seemingly random things.*	**Strategic,** *creates alternate ways to proceed.*	When needing to do something or get somewhere, I consider all possibilities. If none seems right, I create a new one.

As you evaluate career opportunities going forward, consider the following:

- How well do your talents align with the responsibilities of the new role?
- What are the strengths of your prospective supervisor?
- How has your prospective supervisor successfully demonstrated his or her support of subordinates who desired to leverage their talents in and beyond the job responsibilities?

In summary, creating a fulfilling career is closely aligned to your level of intrinsic motivation for whatever direction you choose. Intrinsic motivation, as identified by Kenneth W. Thomas in his book *Intrinsic Motivation at Work: What Really Drives Employee Engagement,* is that fuel within you that generates the effort and creativity for work that you find meaningful.

Many people are willing to offer free advice on what they believe you should be doing, yet believing in yourself and knowing yourself is the most powerful resource for you in leading a strengths-based career.

References

Flade, P., Asplund, J., & Elliot, G. (2015, October 15). *Employees who use their strengths outperform those who don't.* Gallup Workplace. Retrieved from https://www.gallup.com/workplace/236561/employees-strengths-outperform-don.aspx

Office of Personnel Management. (2015). *Engaging the Federal workforce: How to do It & prove it.* Washington, DC: Author. Retrieved from https://admin.govexec.com/media/gbc/docs/pdfs_edit/engaging_the_fede ral_workforce_white_paper.pdf

Wagner, R., & Muller, G. (2019). *Why partners need complementary strengths.* Gallup Workplace. Retrieved from https://news.gallup.com/businessjournal/122237/Why-Partners-Need-Complementary-Strengths.aspx?g_source=link_newsv9&g_campaign=item_124523&g_me dium=copy

----

Monique 'Coach Monique' Betty is president and executive coach of CareerSYNC. She is a Gallup Certified Strengths Coach, an International Coach Federation–credentialed coach, a Certified Executive Coach Specialist, and a certified trainer with the Center for Coaching Certification. Coach Monique is also the author of *7 Guiding Principles to Achieve a Career Advantage* ebook and eLearning course. She works virtually and serves clients around the world.

LEADERSHIP
MYTHS

ll too often, as new and even as experienced leaders, we can become so focused on ensuring that our teams complete tasks and achieve goals that we forget that our teams are composed of human beings with complex emotions and a desire for stability. In times of frequent change and uncertainty, our team's mental and emotional state becomes of the utmost importance. One of the best ways to keep the team moving forward towards success is to project confidence and wield your charisma. When I was the program manager for executive education at my former Federal agency, I was asked to assume management of three Government-wide senior-level leadership development forums. Although the forums had been successfully managed for the past 6 years, there was a lot of angst due to new executive leadership, declining budgets, a lack of communication about the future of the programs, and now me serving as the new program manager. To make matters more difficult, I would be leading an interagency team of GS-13, -14, and -15 training coordinators who had been working together for over 7 years, and at that time I was a 25-year-old GS-9. Can you imagine me walking into our first meeting telling them that I knew what was best and that they should just follow my lead? It would not have gone well for me.

To get in front of what I knew would be a significant challenge, before meeting with the team, I held several meetings with the former program manager to learn as much as possible about the team and team dynamics. I learned who the most influential members were and scheduled one-on-one meetings with them to learn about their challenges, their perceptions of what was taking place, and how I could better support the team. These pre-meetings helped me gain buy-in from key group influencers who would later support me and my decisions. Next, I met with the entire team for another listening session. At the end of that listening session, I assured everyone that I had heard and understood their concerns. I also told them that I believed that it was my job to make them look good, that I would be as transparent as possible, and that I was confident that, with all of their skills and experience, the programs would remain successful for years to come.

Over the next few months, I repeatedly found ways to show the team that they could trust me. I shared whatever information I could tell them, and I was transparent about what I could not share. Over the next 2 years, a great deal of change took place—from the cost of the forums to the location and program format—but because I had used my charisma, projected confidence in the team, and believed the team could overcome any obstacle, the team grew closer than ever. In fact, over my 3 years of leadership, we served approximately 7,500 Federal employees, decreased the overall cost to the customers by 20%, drastically increased revenue, and in one of many firsts, made the programs accessible online from anywhere in the country. These feats could not have been accomplished if I had not been able to use my charisma to project confidence to my team members. Being a charismatic leader gives us the ability to weather storms that non-charismatic leaders would not be able to overcome. Having charisma is like the emergency brake you can pull when the situation is starting to get out of control. Most people understand the power of charisma, but many believe that charisma is something you are born with and that it cannot be learned. That could not be further from the truth. In fact, I teach my clients specific charisma-building strategies that they can incorporate into their everyday behavior.

To continue this conversation on aspects of leadership, I have asked my good friend and business partner, Dr. John Anderson, to share his thoughts on learning from others. Dr. Anderson is an expert leadership development coach and coaches senior leaders across the world.

Leadership from the Perspective of Childhood Lessons

by John E. Anderson, Ph.D.

Leadership skills are key to a successful career. These skills are not tied to position but can be learned early on, even in childhood. The lessons for making your child a leader that are described here can be applied to yourself and can be used to support your peers.

The lessons from our children are often filled with wisdom, and we can learn from them. Take 11-year-old girl Kelsey, who when on a hike with a group of girls through an area of the Rocky Mountains realized (along with the group) that they had taken a wrong trail and were wandering somewhat hopeless—cold, wet, and hungry. One girl sobbed, "They'll never find us, and we're all going to die." Kelsey came forward and said firmly, "I'm not going to die, and I have heard that if you follow a little stream, it empties into a bigger stream and that leads to a town. Let's follow that stream that we saw." All went to the stream and saw that it increased in size, and finally they heard voices from a rescue party. Recounting this story, people tend to say that Kelsey is a born leader. Some people believe that leaders like Kelsey are programmed at birth, while others are destined to follow. However, my work with athletes, college students (Air Force Academy cadets), private- and public-sector employees, and educators has convinced me that leaders are not born, they are made. Women and men who lead organizations and teams are the product of conscientious parents who follow guiding principles that foster a leadership mentality: strength of mind and independent thinking. Their children do not succumb to peer pressure; they follow their own beliefs.

A leadership mentality pays off tomorrow as well as today. Childhood leadership in class and extracurricular activities is an accurate predictor of adult success for both sexes. Some time ago I asked a group of nursery school teachers whether they could identify the leaders among their 4- and 5-year-olds. "Certainly," they replied. These kids were self-confident, treated both adults and peers with respect, shared toys willingly, were good-humored, and showed initiative and curiosity. They were first to start a project, while the other kids watched and then followed their lead. Most of all, their enthusiasm was contagious. Asking several dozen teenage boys and girls about leadership, they described their leaders in almost the same terms: "They smile a lot and seem to feel good about themselves, and they make you feel good." Leadership is always a challenge, and we can find wisdom in the thoughts and behaviors of children. What can you do to help foster a leadership mentality in your children (and perhaps in adults)? Here are several steps to consider.

Be A Booster

Confidence comes from being told "You can do it!", "Well done!" It begins with your child's first steps, as the child ambles toward your congratulatory embrace, scoring a victory and savoring its reward. Each subsequent little success leads to others.

Child Leader

No success is too tiny to be complimented. This does not mean that you fill the air with insincere praise and never provide constructive criticism. When constructive criticism is well placed, a child receives it with understanding. This type of criticism involves instruction and belief in the child's abilities. There was a boy named Rolf who was on our Little League team. He was not a particularly good athlete, yet he gave learning a good effort. I taught Rolf how to field a ground ball, having his glove touch the ground as the ball approached. During a game when Rolf was playing right field, a ball came his way. Anxiety filled Rolf as he bent down with his glove touching the ground (Rolf had missed many of these) and he captured the ball in his glove. In his excitement he threw the ball to one of the other outfielders, all while the boy who hit the ball was running around the bases, and the other outfielder threw the ball to the infield. Rolf was so excited that he had made the play. When he came to the dugout and sat down, I said to him, "That's how to stop those ground balls Rolf—well done! Now learn to throw the ball to the infield." Rolf simply looked at me with a charming smile on his face and said, "Yes, coach!" Rolf has grown up now and is a very successful executive. Provide your children with an environment where there is love and support, accountability and responsibility for their actions, and opportunities for growth.

Let Them Explore

On a nice summer day I was walking in a neighborhood and saw a young girl dig a rock out of her rain-soaked front yard. Her father was on the front porch and she held up the rock saying, "Daddy, look at this beautiful stone I found!" He looked at her disapprovingly: "You are getting all dirty. Get out of that mud." Her face fell and she dropped the stone and then went indoors. This is a simple example, and as you realize, the mark on that child's imagination can last a long time—whereas the mud could have been washed away and the father could have encouraged his daughter to continue exploring. Children (and adults) admire and follow someone who is willing to explore, to rise to challenges. Too often we teach our children to play it safe.

There was a primary school teacher who told me about two boys who arrived in first grade already skilled readers. She asked if they would like to be moved to a more advanced reading program. One boy eagerly agreed while the other said "no thanks." Sadly, the parents supported the decision of the second boy. The teacher said to me, "You can guess which one of those two will go on to be a leader."

Focus on Success

There was a promising 12-year-old gymnast who came to me for help. She had all the skills of a future Olympian, yet was not living up to her capabilities. I handed her four darts and instructed her to toss them at a target across my office. She looked at me nervously and asked, "What if I miss?" Those four words summed up her disappointing career. Instead of focusing on how to succeed, she worried about how to keep from failing.

Persuade your child to think about success, not obstacles. The person who believes in success is the one who inspires others to follow. People have asked me, "When did you become a doctor?" My answer has been, "When I was 9 years old." That was my age when I made that proclamation (probably along with being a fireman, or a truck driver, or whatever). It wasn't that I was particularly smart; it was simply what I wanted to do. As years passed, a very significant number of obstacles confronted me, and I did not lose the commitment to my goal of becoming a doctor. Eventually I made it at age 38. Too often we step in and shield our children from mistakes, their consequences, and the lessons they teach. The child who gains inner resolve is the one who tries, falls short, corrects the errors, and gets up to do it again.

The one who inspires others is the one who rises to the occasion even though she or he might fail. Remember: losers lose and are finished; winners lose and they learn!

Listen to Their Dreams

Your daughter comes home and announces that she wants to be a professional bull rider. Or your son says he's going to be a movie stunt man. Neither squares exactly with the future you had in mind for them, so what do you way? Is it "girls don't do that" or "that's a dangerous job"? Chances are the wannabe bull rider will change her mind and study law, and the daredevil will detour into a business career. Meanwhile, encourage their dreams, however outlandish they seem to you. What counts is the ability to fantasize and think about what might make the fantasies come true. Leaders have been described as having a vision with the ability to explain it to others and influence them to follow the path to attaining the vision. Children often dream, and parents (like executives/supervisors) can either offer encouragement or find ways to dissolve the dreams.

Ask "What If?"

On a playground in our neighborhood, I watched a little girl working to climb the first step of a slide. Her legs were a bit too short and she ran to her mother asking to be lifted up. Instead of picking her up and placing her on the ladder, the mother asked, "How can you reach it?" The little girl fussed a little bit and then saw the wagon that had helped carry her to the playground. She looked at mom and said, "I'll use the wagon, OK?" The mom nodded, and the girl pulled the wagon over to the ladder and climbed on up. Possibility thinking is another characteristic of successful leaders. Those who examine a problem and show others how to solve it invariably lead the way. Encourage your child (and workers) to ask, "What if I did this?"

Give Them a Chance

Leadership will be sharpened with experience and practice. Check out Little Leaguers, Scouts, and kids in little theater shows—children who find opportunities to get involved and practice skills, which nurtures leadership skills. Enroll your children in sports teams, Scouts, church groups, community organizations, and other activities that give them opportunities to lead, follow, and gain experience in dealing with others. Let your children strive for leadership in their own areas of interest. Some kids lead on the playground and some in the classroom. Not everyone can be class president or even wants to be. However, a talented writer can become editor of the school newspaper, or president of the chess club, or a guiding light in a robotics club. Operating in an area where one feels at home builds confidence, a foundation for leadership! Schools often give children an opportunity to chair a session, to bring other children into a discussion, to keep a team focused on its objective, and to lead. Parents can practice such skills around the family dinner table, letting children lead a discussion on a topic of their choice, gathering the varied comments, and then summarizing the discussion. Our children want to succeed, and it happens most often when we give them a chance.

Be a Campaign Manager

One very helpful ingredient for people in general is the ability to smile. Teaching your children the advantages of this simple behavior is a positive in their life. Children who greet people, in and out of their circle of friends, are often recognized as potential leaders. There was a young man who had a difficult time connecting with people in his workplace (yes, he was older), and he was their supervisor. He was a nice person who seemed somewhat grumpy. After he and I discussed his situation, we agreed that he would simply add a behavior; the behavior he added was a smile. After 3 months, he and I met again and the difference in him was noticeable. His people wondered what had come over him because he was so different. Yet the only change to his behaviors was the smile. Your children will learn quickly, through your campaigning with them, that a genuinely positive approach to others will help them throughout life. Give them suggestions about voice level, strength of expression, eye contact, and positive, can-do word choices.

Develop a Positive Brain

Children can be hard on each other, saying and doing things that interrupt parents' efforts to build positivity. Although this is often a challenge, parents can do three things to help build a positive brain: (1) repetition, frequent emphasis on the use of positive word choices and positive behaviors; (2) feedback, providing frequent feedback for desired language and behaviors; and (3) gratitude, teaching children what gratitude is and how to express it.

In the end, it's not your words (although they can help) but your example that counts. If you make negative remarks about your neighbors, coworkers, or family members, you can't expect your daughter or son to develop respect for others. If you frequently drive over the speed limit or simply complain a lot, you can't expect your children to accept responsibility or develop positivity. Studies of leaders have shown that their parents exhibited leadership qualities, though often in unrecognized ways. They considered community service important, making a point to help others, and had dreams for their families—often couched in terms of values and standards, rather than material gain. Put to the test in challenging times, they displayed inner strength that helped the family show their resilience. Nutrition experts say that if you want a healthy child, then provide a healthy diet. This is good physical nutrition. The idea that what you put in is what you get back also applies to good mental nutrition, the character development of a child. The love and attention that parents direct to their child returns in the form of inner strength and confidence and translates to leadership.

Conclusion

Remember the verse *"All I really need to know I learned in kindergarten"* by Robert Fulghum? This is a classical piece that teaches us to pay attention to lessons we can learn from children. Each of the above "steps" for developing child leaders applies to building leadership in our adult lives. In the Federal Government, a leadership skills 360 survey examines Federal executive behaviors in 28 competencies. Review of 1,000 of these surveys showed that two competencies stood out for executive performance: integrity/honesty and interpersonal skills. We have found that when employees trust their leader and are able to communicate openly with them, that leader tends to excel.

We constantly remind individuals in leadership positions that *human beings seek to be affirmed, not denigrated.* These affirmations result in building the confidence of workers, and greater confidence results in more calculated risk-taking behaviors, which in turn results in growth for individuals, teams, and organizations. The "steps" for children noted above, along with a focus on the competencies mentioned, help build an optimistic culture for organizations. Leadership is always a challenge, and by returning to our childhood days, you will find pearls of wisdom that will help grow your own leadership skills.

John E. Anderson, Ph.D., is the founder and principal for the Center for Sports Psychology (https://www.c4sp.com/). He was a tenured associate professor at the U.S. Air Force Academy and has provided performance-based leadership skills for private- and public-sector executives, Olympic coaches, and athletes and helped guide programs for the Center for Creative Leadership. He currently resides in Monument, Colorado.

COLLECTIVE PROBLEM SOLVING

I know that you and I are a lot alike because you are reading this book. We are a member of a relatively small group of individuals who take control of our surroundings to ensure that we always reach our goals. We progressed through our careers by not only building strategic relationships, but by being the person that others rely on when something needs to be done. We are the people who everyone looks to for solutions when there is a problem. And, if all of those things are true, you might be one of the many leaders who become excessively stressed trying to find, and implement, the best solutions to the problems you are given. If that last statement strikes a chord, I know exactly how you feel because I felt the same way years back—that is, until I realized that it was not my job to solve everyone's problems. Let me explain.

The higher you go within the organization, the more complex problems become. In fact, years back I had positioned myself to secure a senior leadership promotion I had been eyeing for a while. The job would be completely different than my previous positions, but I was confident that my ability to quickly learn new skills would help me be successful. Unfortunately, I was wrong. After just a few months on the job, I found myself completely overwhelmed and I felt like I was consistently drinking from a firehose. In the past I had prided myself on being a problem solver— you know, the guy who could parachute into a situation, analyze it, make some key decisions that would solve the problem, and jump on the next plane to the next problem. However, this approach was not working in this new position. The primary reason was because the scope and complexities of the problems were just too different than the scope and complexities of the problems I had previously dealt with. Thus, every time I tried solving a problem, I was quickly told that my solution would not work because of XYZ.

This was very disheartening and I started to question whether I had made the right career move. One day I had a career-changing realization. I thought to myself: There is no way that I will ever know as much about these topics as the other people in the room. They were all trained in their respective topics and had been working in those areas for years. So, I decided that instead of trying to solve the teams' problems, I would focus my effort on helping the teams solve their own problems. I basically became a facilitator. Whenever a new problem arose, I would decide who needed to be at the table, ask probing questions to make sure that all possible variables were discussed, track who made commitments, and ensure that the commitments were met. It was wonderful! I no longer felt the heavy burden of always having to be the person with the right answer. Funny enough, this approach had two additional benefits:

1. Because the team created the solution, I did not have to spend nearly as much time gaining buy-in and commitment for implementation.
2. Because I was the one bringing the teams together and facilitating the discussions, everyone viewed me as the group leader!

Making this one mindset change resulted in less stress and an increased perception of leadership ability.

I share this story to debunk the myth that effective leaders have to solve problems on their own. I have coached senior leaders from many Federal agencies, and all too often they torment themselves with this unhelpful myth. I want you to learn from my mistakes and understand that the primary job of the leader in problem-solving situations is to do 6 things:

- Make sure that the right people are in the room
- Empower the team to solve the problem
- Ask probing questions
- Encourage team members to contribute to the discussion

- Ensure a decision is made
- Provide accountability to ensure everyone completes their commitments on time

I have asked a good friend and former colleague, Dr. Andrew Rahaman, to further discuss the importance of addressing organizational challenges collectively through asking great questions. Dr. Rahaman is a very respected practitioner in the fields of organizational learning, leadership, and change management with over 26 years of Federal Government experience.

Leaders Need Constant Development: Peer-to-Peer Learning and Coaching

by Andrew Rahaman, Ed.D.

"**We are all Government leaders**." What a bold and yet proactive statement given the Government's structure is quite visibly hierarchical in nature and yet must rely on small, agile teams to create organizational change. A Government leader is not solely about being hierarchically in charge. Furthermore, it is impossible to be the only expert solving rapidly evolving organizational challenges. Consequently, the best Government leaders recognize the need for new ways of thinking from all levels of the organization; the need to understand the enterprise perspective and impact of solving one organizational challenge; and the social contract that requires high levels of employee engagement/development in order to retain the best and brightest staff members. These leaders encourage shared leadership at all levels. Hence, leadership can be viewed through the practice of being able to create and articulate a vision; align thinking, resources, and effort towards that vision; and engage people in ways that develop commitment by those directly, and indirectly, impacted by the outcome of the vision.

In the quest to develop enterprise leaders, employee engagement is a must. However, according to Gallup research, and as most of our readers will attest to, less than 25% of employees receive meaningful feedback that helps them develop. Sadly, even less than that agree that their performance is managed in a way that motivates them to do their very best. This has serious implications for harnessing engagement and driving organizational performance.

Reframe Development

One solution is to reframe the role of the manager from solely giving feedback to creating a system for performance development that involves all staff within the office. This change inherently embraces inquiry over advocacy, reflection, and action.

The truth is that we grow and develop in the company of others. So what better way to unlock collaborative leadership and learning than by working together to address the challenges the organization is facing. This can be achieved through peer-to-peer learning and coaching. Effective peer-to-peer learning and coaching unlocks the capacity of those involved and empowers them to create real-time learning interaction on real organizational challenges that need broad-based perspectives. Peer-to-peer learning is Socratic by nature. That is, it is nondirective, and peers discover solutions via questions and conversations with others who have similar challenges. In this way, peer-to-peer learning lends itself to developing collaborative leadership at all levels of the organization.

When I think of peer-to-peer learning, I often think of learning in action or a variant of what is known as "action learning." Peer-to-peer learning shares important tenets to developing leaders by sharing experiences and solutions within the context of the organization. Six of these shared tenets are as follows:

1. The process recognizes that feedback is hard to take. Often, feedback is perceived as veiled criticism that results in feeling "less than" and/or being micromanaged. Peer-to-peer learning and coaching puts everyone on equal ground by asking peers to share their suggestions via questions to reframe the thinking of the original problem and allow a multitude of possible solutions rather than coming out with one solution. This level of concurrent sharing of questions ultimately leads to concurrent leadership. That is, there is no one single person with all of the right answers, and responsibility rests on the entire group's participation. Importantly, as questions and solutions come from different people around the organization, participants start to develop a broader picture of the enterprise and how the issues affect different business units. This level of enterprise thinking develops people to think beyond their "silos" and to understand the perspectives of other units.

2. The learning is focused and acquired in the context of a real issue facing the organization. In this way, everyone becomes invested in the issue, takes ownership, and comes to see themselves as partners. We know that when people are given a stake in the problem, including the implementation of its solution, their commitment increases.

3. Learning is collective in nature through the sharing of information. Individuals each bring their perspective or knowledge to the issues. By inviting others to share their perspective, first through questions and then through solutions, they increase the range of opportunities available to solve the issue. By sharing, the group collectively comes up with views that emanate from a process of people working together, not one person mobilizing action.

4. Invested individuals move from quick and straightforward problem solving (e.g., "You tell me your problem and I give you an answer") to a thorough analysis that reflects on the cause of the problem, any feedback from stakeholders, assumptions being made, and approaches to solving the problem. This, ultimately, broadens their perspective and willingness to be open to others' way of thinking. In essence, they start to reframe the problem from an organic understanding to look deeper into the causes and effects.

5. Participants develop compassion and unity. Fear can be reduced by openly and willingly asking questions in a nonthreatening, nonevaluative way. Peer-to-peer coaching and learning builds partnerships as people discuss their goals, enable questions, and share perspectives. As you probably know, as we talk about our goals, write them down, and are held accountable for reaching them, the chances of us reaching our goals dramatically increase. Collaboration can lead to compassion; as participants are willing to talk about their issues, listen to others' questions, and take in suggestions, they begin to value each other's viewpoints and each other even more. In other words, they start to practice compassion for one another by seeing themselves as interconnected through democratic participation.

6. Individuals hold each other accountable for follow through of the original issue and, more importantly, for each other's development. Peer-to-peer coaching and learning helps people create bonds of trust. And, those who trust others, and are trusted by others, tend to follow through on obligations.

You might be wondering, "how can I do all of this?" Here is a way I recently used peer-to-peer learning and coaching with a group to broaden the way people saw their workplace challenges and to build interdependency to a common strategic objective.

1. Each person identified a workplace challenge and wrote it down on a flip chart in one to two sentences for everyone to see.

2. We went around the room and asked clarifying questions starting with four categories:

    a. **Identifying the problem** by understanding where the person is now and the impact of the problem at that moment. For instance, we asked questions such as: What is the current impact of the issue on organizational goals or relationships? What has happened so far? Who is involved? What is not working?
    b. **Asking future-forward questions** that create a preferred state. For instance: If you were to make a change, what would this look like in 3 months? What would success look like to you and the organization? How might this be perceived by others in the organization?
    c. **Creating actions that** identify progress and next steps toward the goals. For instance: How will you know you are being successful? What would a solution (to your workplace challenge) look like 2 months from now? What is one thing you could do within the first week?
    d. **Build confidence and support** so people continue to move forward. People eed to be encouraged to change to try and to reinforce new behaviors. For instance: When would you like to meet again as a group to talk about how our new behavior is impacting others? What will you be proud of after you start your new behavior? How can we support your efforts?

3. After going around the room asking questions, we gave the problem presenter an opportunity to reframe the question. The reason we do this is because when others ask us open-ended learning-based questions, we tend to incorporate them into part of the solution, and we know that if we get the right question, we are closer to the solution. Hence, the questions often contain kernels of the solution or point us toward a solution that we probably had not been thinking of. When the problem presenter is able to reframe the question and identify a few ideas, everyone in the peer-to-peer learning circle is given the opportunity to visit each flip chart and write down additional questions, ideas, and possible solutions. This important step serves as a way to unite the group by increasing investment in each other's challenge.

4. At a predetermined time later, each person comes back to the group and debriefs action steps he or she has taken on the workplace challenge.

When managers create an environment that engages others in the development of others through peer-to-peer coaching and learning, the team learns more about the organization through these perspectives; they learn how to actively listen and ask learning-based questions; they empower others to connect across the organization; they grow as individuals and contributing team members who can articulate a vision; they build trust as people realize they are all in this together; and they align and engage the team in a way that harnesses the social contract of employee engagement.

So, the next time you have a staff meeting or want to support professional development, consider an activity like this in lieu of having each person report on the issues that they alone are working on. Besides all of its benefits, it is a fun activity.

"Action comes about if, and only if, we find a discrepancy between what we are experiencing and what we want to experience." —*Philip J. Runkel*

Andrew Rahaman, Ed.D., has worked nationally and internationally with leaders and organizations of all sizes in the public and private sectors, including 26 years in Federal Government. He is an executive in residence at American University, where he teaches graduate courses on organizational learning, leadership, change, and teams for the university's Key Executive Education Programs, which are tailored to the U.S. Government. Rahaman is also on the staff of the Center for Creative Leadership and past chair of the U.S. affiliate of the World Institute for Action Learning. Andrew specializes in executive coaching, onboarding, organizational culture assessment, and the design and delivery of leadership development programs. He can be reached at rahamanaa@gmail.com or Rahaman@american.edu. Follow him on Twitter @ProfA_Rahaman

THE IMPORTANCE OF EXECUTIVE PRESENCE

T he Secretary of the Department of the Interior had just finished an all-employee meeting when I noticed the Director of the U.S. National Park Service (NPS) exiting the room by himself. Seeing this as an opportune time, I quickly introduced myself and asked if he and I could meet sometime within the next 2 months. To my delight, he said yes. On the day of the meeting, I walked through the Director's corridor, past two men in suits, and introduced myself to the receptionist. After waiting a couple minutes, the three of us were escorted to the Director's office. The two men introduced themselves as very senior-level leaders in the NPS and handed me two briefing documents they had brought for me. The meeting began with me thanking the Director for his time and sharing that I was interested in learning more about the challenges the NPS was facing. After the group shared a few of their most pressing challenges, the Director asked me how I would go about addressing those challenges. Less than 20 minutes into our conversation, the Director asked me if I would be interested in working for the NPS. Of course, I said that I would greatly appreciate the opportunity, and the rest is history.

Almost 6 months after joining the NPS, one of the men who had been in the room decided to share with me the story of that day from his perspective. First, when I reached out to the Director to schedule the meeting the Director could not remember who I was—only that I had worked within the Office of the Secretary. Thus, he asked two of his senior-level leaders to join our meeting because they thought that I might have been a senior-level political appointee. This was assumed because of how I had handled myself in my initial conversation with the Director, in addition to my initiative in requesting a one-on-one meeting with the Director. The senior leader also shared with me the impression I made when I arrived for the meeting that day. He explained that there was "something about me" that made them feel that I belonged there. It wasn't until 15 minutes into the meeting that they realized that I was not some heavy-hitting political operative, but a young professional looking for his next opportunity. He said that they were so impressed with my bravery and proactiveness that they knew that I would be a valuable member of their team.

Surprisingly enough, that was not the first time or the last time that I walked into a room and was assumed to be a senior-level official. This skill, which can be learned and which I teach to my mentoring clients, is called executive presence. Having executive presence is essential for anyone hoping to climb the ranks within the Federal Government. That is why I spend a significant portion of my programs helping my clients further develop it. To speak more on this topic, I reached out to the author of the phenomenal reputation-building book, *Build Your Reputation: Grow Your Personal Brand for Career and Business Success,* Rob Brown. Rob, a UK-based international speaker and authority on personal marketing and business reputations, is an expert in the area, and you will learn a great deal from his chapter.

Unlocking your Executive Presence

by: Rob Brown

If you're in any kind of leadership, management or trusted advisor role, you need gravitas and personal impact. If you have to sell, persuade or influence, you need executive presence. It produces the kind of aura that makes people listen and most importantly, act. This chapter will provide you with a number of concrete steps you can take to increase your EP.

Here are 3 of Rob's 7 common situations where you might need a healthy dose of EP:

- To win backing for an idea. Every idea, every objective, every vision needs selling. With EP, you throw a certain weight of authority behind it that makes people more likely to accept, obey and even like it.

- To gain help or buy-in for a project or initiative. You can't do all you need to do 'on your own' so you need others. Your ability to negotiate and get big things done will dictate your success. EP is the 'secret sauce' that draws people into your schemes and plans so that they're fully on board.

- To change the culture in your team or office. Often you inherit a set up that is not of your making You need to change hearts and minds on a cultural level. A strong perceived EP will get you taken seriously and make it more likely that you can drive the change you seek.

4 of Rob's 14 Executive Presence Tips to Advance Your Career

- <u>Avoid feeling entitled.</u> Just because you're smart, driven and good at what you do doesn't mean you deserve a promotion or corner office. Your EP will also play a huge part in how far you'll go, so get over yourself and add EP to your undoubted competence.

- <u>Think beyond performance.</u> Don't just think that by doing a good job or hitting your targets, you'll get promoted. Beyond your actual performance, there are many not-so-obvious skills you'll need in your arsenal to ensure you get everything you're working so hard for.

- <u>Play to your strengths.</u> Look at these elements of EP that are critical to career development and leadership: grace under fire, decisiveness, emotional intelligence and the ability to read a room, integrity and authenticity, a vision that inspires others, and a stellar reputation. No human being can get an A+ in all of these. It's about avoiding the behaviors that get you struck off the list. Figure out your natural strengths and use them well for the fastest possible progress.

- <u>Be always 'on'.</u> The term 'extreme job' is now used to describe the new 24/7 workday. You're always on show and always being judged. Everything you put on social media defines you. You leak between personal and work life. Stay mindful of all you do and say.

4 of Rob's 30 Common Signs that You Have Executive Presence

- <u>You command respect when you speak.</u> It's not that you are demanding, loud or insistent. You are merely confident in your position and you naturally assert your views. And you engage the audience well so they are receptive to those views.
- <u>You draw out alternative views before acting.</u> For you, there is no waffling or endless meetings to make a decision. You have the ability to gather enough information without having to endlessly study the problem. You are comfortable making decisions without each and every detail. You would rather take a bit of a risk and capitalize on a situation than to have a perfect solution too late.

- <u>You are calm and in control under stress.</u> Adversity seems to bring out your best leadership ability. You click into command central mode and 'boss' situations in times of crisis. You're good at issuing directives and processing data. You can go to the heart of the matter and drive for a practical solution. You are the calm in the eye of the storm.

- <u>You have deep knowledge.</u> Sounding uneducated or uninformed negatively impacts the way others perceive you. If you've got EP, then you'll seem to know the stuff that needs knowing. You'll analyze well, have a decent grasp of the details and also a sense of the bigger picture. You can go deep with key topics and feel assured in your particular areas of expertise. You push back and challenge where appropriate, and appear solid in your understanding of what's important in any given situation.

3 of Rob's 7 Interesting Facts About Executive Presence

- <u>EP shows up in very different people.</u> Very diverse people have been shown to exude EP. Warren Buffet, Oprah Winfrey and Steve Jobs have it. Bill Clinton and Tony Blair have it. Margaret Thatcher had it. Graham Norton and Jonathan Ross have it. All very different personalities. All have that confidence and composure that ensures a connection with others.

- <u>EP is not about charisma.</u> It's not about commanding the room. If it was, you'd always aim to become the center of attention. You don't have to be the most gregarious or outspoken person in the room to demonstrate EP. It's not about being an extrovert. Some people with huge EP are actually very shy. You can still command a room from a position of stillness and relative silence.

- <u>EP is age indifferent.</u> It's assumed that gravitas comes with age, but if you are intentional, you can accelerate your development of EP qualities at any age.

3 of Rob's 15 Top Tips to Use Words for More Executive Presence

- <u>Cut out non-words.</u> These are utterances that mean nothing. "Uhms" and errs kill you in conversations. They show hesitance and a reluctance to yield the stage to others. You say non-words to tell people you're still talking and still thinking. You're saying 'don't interrupt - I'm still going here.' You're also buying time while you articulate your thoughts. Again, a show of weakness. There is a better way to do that.

- <u>Stop with the fillers.</u> These fluffy fillers dilute your message and lessen any impact:
  - o I think
  - o You know
  - o Sort of
  - o Kind of
  - o Like
  - o Just
  - o You know what I mean

Take these out of your vocabulary. They undermine your EP and don't add anything to your core message.

- <u>Set up your insights.</u> If you're going to say something impactful, tee it up properly. That way people sense something good is coming. Try some of these phrases before you say something profound or insightful:

1. Here's how I see this
2. Here's a thought
3. Here's my best thinking on this
4. Want to know what I think?
5. Here's what's happening here
6. Guess what?
7. We're missing something here
8. You might be missing the point
9. Here's something nobody's thought about
10. Wait a moment
11. How about this?
12. Let me come in here
13. I'll just say this
14. Stop for a second

15. Let's just pause for a moment
16. Hang on a minute
17. Something's not right here
18. Here's what's going on here
19. Wait a moment
20. The most important thing here is this

These are statements of intent and power. They sound and feel different to what's gone on before, and they tend to get people's attention. Just make sure that the next thing you say after these is strong enough to justify the set up. Otherwise you're set up for a fall.

6 of Rob's 50 EP Top Tips

- <u>Know the politics.</u> If you want EP, be in the business of making allies, not enemies. You need buy-in and consensus. Pay attention to workplace etiquette and politics. Stay out of squabbles but get to know the personal agendas of those involved. Show respect to all, regardless of their rank or station. Find out what others want and what makes them tick.

- <u>Write well.</u> Strong writing skills are foundational to building EP. Hone your writing skills because your personal brand is on show every time you show up in print. Emails, letters, texts, social media posts and proposals should mirror your 'in person' communication. Go easy on exclamation marks and emojis. Emulate the styles of strong written communicators and get some coaching in this area if needed.

- <u>Keep it real.</u> You're aiming to be the best possible version of you. Being genuine is one of the most magnetic and memorable qualities anyone can possess. While it's good to admire and follow the example of role models, you can't be someone you aren't. Nor should you even try. Besides, faking it is obvious to others and exhausting for you.

- <u>Minimize impulsive behavior.</u> People with EP rarely get angry. They have emotional resilience. Under pressure and in challenging situations, they stay cool. If you find that in the eye of the storm, you tend to react with fear or impulse, you need more self control. Set the tone. Stay composed. Gravitas is a depth of personality that doesn't fret, worry or over-react. No matter the situations, never let your emotions overpower your intelligence.

- Cultivate substance. This is the depth and weight behind your style. The opposite to superficial, if you like. It's made up of your social presence, demeanor and gravitas in leadership situations. It's wisdom. It's self-assurance. It's having the game to back up your claim. If you have a fine style but little substance, they may be perceived as too showy. The Americans say 'empty suits.' The Brits say 'all style and no substance.' You've got to have weight behind your punches rather than just dancing around the ring looking good but achieving nothing.
- Tell more stories. Your ability to weave a narrative is vital to your success. Stories are real. They are powerful and memorable. They light up your points with meaning and intent. They give evidence for your supremacy and they back up your arguments. Examples, case studies and anecdotes are all powerful in convincing others that you're 'the real deal' and have true EP.

To learn more about Rob Brown and his products please visit https://www.youtube.com/watch?reload=9&v=rGbsb6aXbzc and you can purchase his book, "Build Your Reputation," at https://www.amazon.com/Build-Your-Reputation-Personal-Business/dp/1119274451

*Reprinted with permission from Rob Brown, featured TEDx speaker and bestselling author of Build Your Reputation.

RELATIONSHIP BUILDING

W hen I was just 24 years old, I met someone who would become one of my closest friends and mentors. At the time I met him, he had already served the American public in some of the most influential Senior Executive Service roles within the Government. One of the first things he taught me was that the most successful Government employees do not rely on job announcements to find their next opportunity. He shared that he had not secured a job via USAJOBS in over 20 years. Yes, he may have submitted his resume to USAJOBS a few times, but that was just a formality. He had secured all of his promotions before the job announcement had even hit the street.

Being a member of a diverse community, he stressed the importance of building strong relationships with key individuals, as well as always being respectful and considerate of all people regardless of their grade. I later expounded on this concept by thinking of networking as building a strong defense and offense. A strong offensive network will help you identify opportunities to grow and will advance your career/life goals. On the other hand, having a strong defensive network will protect you when people try to sabotage or otherwise negatively impact your career. Having a strong offense and a strong defense is extremely important as you reach for more senior-level Government positions.

Over the years, I have found that there are four types of people:

- People who do not want to network
- People who want to network, but do not know how
- People who actively network by attending random happy hours and other social gatherings
- People who have high career aspirations and want to develop a strategic networking plan that will drastically increase the probability that they will reach their goals

Because my clients are generally focused on reaching the GS-13/14/15 or Senior Executive Service, most of the strategies I promote are focused on the fourth category. If you are interested in learning more about networking strategies, you can find useful tools on my YouTube channel (https://www.youtube.com/alextremble) and subscribe to my *GPS Success Strategies* newsletter (http://alextremble.com/).

One of the most creative networking professionals I know is Kitty Wooley. I met Kitty, author of *Boundary Spanning in Practice,* almost 8 years ago and have continually been impressed with her ability to build *real* relationships with senior-level officials within numerous Federal agencies. When she was a Federal employee, all of her assignments were inside one agency, but because of her interests in relationship building and idea sharing, she started her own organization called Senior Fellows and Friends. Her events were attended by some of the most senior-level employees within the Federal Government, and she quickly gained a reputation among influential leaders in the learning and development realm. Kitty and I have partnered on multiple workshops, networking webinars, and even articles. Because we take slightly different views on networking, I have asked her to share some of her thoughts and recommendations.

Feeling Unrecognized or Underappreciated? Start Doing This.

by Kitty Wooley

Now and then, there's a solid contributor who just can't seem to progress within the organization, for reasons that have nothing to do with either performance or conduct. When this happens, it's discouraging for the individual and a net loss for the organization. Although this can happen at any age, it may be especially devastating for newer employees who haven't yet developed the tacit knowledge that would enable them to consider a wider variety of next steps. I've seen people in this situation go straight to job hunting, but that is rarely the best first option (unless you've just realized that you hate everything about your current employer, in which case, job hunt away). If you want to have a greater impact and set yourself up for future success—in your current workplace and elsewhere—then do this.

1. Pause and Reflect on Your Commitment

Why are you working *here*? "Because I needed a job" only works for so long, even though it stays true at some level for most of us. At some point, you have to develop a better reason or work becomes an unrelenting, demoralizing grind. Over time, the pay is important, but the meaning is critical. Most people I know find meaning by choosing to believe that they are *making a difference.* Many have chosen to make a difference through some form of Government service. Other people make a difference in such varied ways as probing the boundaries of the known world through academic research, designing instructional materials that help workforces improve corporate and nonprofit performance, starting small businesses, and so on. If you can figure out what you're committed to, not for all time, but at least for now, you can develop next steps that lead to a more satisfying work life with greater impact.

2. Envision Win/Win Scenarios

It's almost always possible to reframe thinking so that everybody gets something they want. What does that look like? See if you can "translate" this brief example into your world.

I work for the Department of XYZ as a grants management specialist. My particular position involves providing technical support to local organizations that are planning to apply for grants announced by my Agency. I also help current grantees understand and comply with their reporting and financial obligations, so that they demonstrate administrative capability and the grant money can keep flowing. If I go above and beyond the minimum to serve current and prospective grantees well,

- **They win.** *They have the funding they need at the right time and are enabled to pursue their public mission. Staff contacts appreciate my professionalism and may even think more highly of my Agency, because the Agency has made it easier for them to apply for or administer the grant.*
- **The Agency wins.** *The grant programs I support run more smoothly because I am on the ball. The money flows on time, is used for the intended purpose, and can be properly accounted for. My Agency's leaders are much less likely to get angry calls or see the program appear in the news for the wrong reason.*
- **I win.** *Not only have I played a part in delivering grant funding that could improve conditions for a portion of this country's 326 million people, but I did it to the best of my ability, represented my department ably, and made a point to learn something new in the process. I'm refining my practice and becoming more skillful—and thus more valuable to an astute employer—all the time.*

Win/win scenarios like the above occur when some commonality is found among the players' interests. Such alignment is not always obvious. Whenever you are able to see potential win/win scenarios and make them visible to everyone else who has a stake in what you're working on, you demonstrate a skill that is central to eliciting cooperation and reaching goals. Even if the scenarios you envisioned don't come to pass, you keep working with integrity and a positive attitude. Those are attractive qualities; they *attract* the kind of attention that will encourage you and help you move forward. Use the same kind of win/win thinking as you broaden your network, so that it's never just about you. Generosity has a way of attracting new opportunity.

3. Strategically Broaden Your Network
You do not need anyone else's permission to connect with others who may be able to help you, unless you believe someone else owns you. If you

have unconsciously given that power to your boss or anyone else, take it back. Unless you want to be recognized for the wrong reasons, don't be a jerk about this. Simply begin growing your autonomy and ability to think, decide, and act.

Use common sense: when you're at work, whether at the office or working remotely, you are obligated to do the work you accepted when you were hired. Fulfilling that obligation demonstrates your integrity and sometimes even your promotability. But, that does not mean you cannot go beyond your job requirements and connect with others who are doing different work elsewhere.

4. Do Advance Preparation

Make sure you're keeping track of your accomplishments as you go—including those that are not in your performance plan if you think they're significant. Writing them down and storing the written record somewhere accessible will give you raw material that you can use to gain perspective, better understand what you've been doing and why it matters, and see your talents in a new light. That will motivate you to keep repeating the three steps above.

When you are not on the clock—for example, on your lunch break, before or after work, or on weekends—start identifying people who might be in the center of the following diagram:

You can do anything related to broadening your network during the workday once you are able to make a convincing case for the ways in which it will benefit the organization. Until you understand how to do that, it may be better to do this preparation when you're off work. Conversations that occur with people in the center will help you keep developing your thinking, craft, and difference-making in a direction that you can travel for a long time with optimism and vigor. As you develop the habit of initiating such conversations, you build a *career engine* as you broaden your network.

To identify people to talk to, begin noticing those who make you feel energetic and positive, whose results and way of working you admire. They should be among your target conversations, regardless of their organizational affiliation, grade, or rank.

5. Start Making Connections

One at a time, ask each person on your list whether he or she would be willing to have a career conversation with you. If the person is a senior executive with a broad span of control, help the executive become interested enough to say yes by asking about his or her work. What aspect of it interests you enough to ask about? Of course, *this means you have to get curious, do your homework, and find out what the person does and is trying to accomplish.*

My experience and observations have shown that most people will say yes to a sincere request, especially if you've demonstrated some understanding and savvy. What does that look like?

Example 1: If you're seeking an information interview with an executive, it's safe to assume that he or she has a scheduler. Make an effort to find out the scheduler's email address and send the request to that person instead of the executive, if you can. The scheduler may ask you for the questions you want to ask the boss. That's rarely the power trip it may seem to be; you are just helping the scheduler keep the boss organized. The questions will be relayed to the executive, giving him or her a quick way to decide whether or not to spend time with you. Organizational "tops" inhabit a complex environment and need to use their time well. Since the development of talent is often a priority, and your request has shown that you are somewhat innovative and squared away, the answer will often be yes.

Example 2: If you're seeking an information interview with a supervisor or middle manager, be aware that he or she is being pulled in many different directions. What questions could you ask that would stimulate free-flowing conversation and motivate the person to teach you something you can use later or even send you to a peer who's a better fit for you? Be very careful not to use the conversation to job hunt, although you could indicate your willingness to move if asked.

Example 3: If you're seeking an information interview with an individual contributor, get clear on what aspect of that person's expertise most intrigues you and why. This will help you avoid wasting the person's time. Is it specific subject matter expertise? Is it the ability to stay relevant and keep being consulted, no matter who's in the executive suite this year?

Keep in mind that any of these people could also help you source developmental opportunities in the future, such as finding a detail, shadowing assignment, or mentoring arrangement that fits you like a glove. Opportunities that are a good fit can provide momentum, resulting in amazing career opportunity.

Save the questions you ask and the answers you receive, so that you can feed the most satisfying ones back into your preparation next time. Keep a "living file" that also includes your accomplishments on your phone or in a

Dropbox folder or personal hard drive. Your continued practice will gradually enlarge your comfort zone and make it easier to connect with colleagues in other organizational components and layers. The goal is to integrate what you're learning with what you already know and then put it to use, with as little wasted motion as possible.

If someone says no, <u>do not take it personally</u>. Move on at once. If the message was "not now, but later," put a reminder on your calendar and try again later.

6. Close the Loop

Thank everyone you talk to, by email or handwritten note, right away after the conversation unless you're in the hospital or in the midst of a crisis (in which case, thank them as soon as you can). Put some effort into it; you'll be remembered as that rare employee who bothered. If possible, include one thing you took away from the conversation: a story you were told, a point that was made, how skillfully an interruption was handled, and so on.

For example, a conversation I had with a retired Navy jet pilot who had become an information technology executive was a sterling instance of executive presence. I appeared in his outer office at 5:00 pm as previously arranged with his scheduler. The scheduler had left for the day, and the executive was on what sounded like an urgent but nonconfidential conference call in his office. He poked his head out the door and motioned for me to wait, then withdrew again, leaving the door open. Twenty minutes later, the call ended, he came out, and we began what stretched into an hour-long conversation. I don't remember the questions I asked or his answers. However, I'll never forget two things:

- The way he left the door open so that I could hear his end of the conversation, demonstrating trust and his judgment that what I would learn from exposure to his operational style outweighed the need for privacy.
- His generosity in extending what was to have been a brief conversation to an hour at the end of a long day. The man was showing me a leader worthy of followers.

In Conclusion

All of the strategies described above have been road-tested for years. Take what you can use and leave the rest. Most important is to develop a habit of thinking and acting—not waiting for perfection, but summoning as much discernment as possible. Your repeated practice of the craft of connection will expand your comfort zone so that you can be relaxed and effective more of the time. Be sure to stay aligned with your organization's direction, remembering that it's never just about you, but it always ought to include you. If you do this, you will be seen and appreciated by others who are able to recognize your unique talent and offer you endless opportunity to make a difference, while you make a living.

_____

Kitty Wooley, M.A., PMP, spent 19 years at the U.S. Department of Education, retiring in 2013. Her first position involved a transition from college financial aid director to Federal institutional review specialist in San Francisco, where her team examined college financial aid operations in four States to ensure that billions of dollars intended to help students pay for college were doing just that. Later work in Washington, D.C., included data analysis and risk management, business intelligence and decision support, stakeholder outreach, translation of IT issues into plain language, and design and execution of interagency mentoring experiences for executive branch budget staff. The Senior Fellows and Friends network she began convening after work in 2003 continues to foster an atmosphere of trust among public service leaders at every level. If you have questions, please contact her at kittywooley5@gmail.com.

UNDERSTANDING AND WORKING WITH POLITICAL APPOINTEES

The last 3 to 6 months of the presidential campaign are absolutely critical for politically savvy Federal Government leaders. One reason is because this is when they begin finalizing their personal transition strategies and plans.

Whether you are leading an agency, an organization, or a program, there are two ways to deal with a political transition. The first way is to hope that the winning party will support your program—or will not care about it and will simply leave you and your program alone. This is what most people do. But you and I know that hope is not a strategy, and passively hoping for the best is not a plan. The second approach to dealing with a new Administration is to think very strategically about both possible election outcomes and develop plans to demonstrate how your program or interests align with the best interests of the Administration. This approach will enhance the likelihood that the new Administration will support your programs.

To further discuss issues of political transitions and political appointees, I have partnered with political powerhouse Michael O'Bannon, Fortune 500 lobbyist Ryan Martin, and experienced public- and private-sector leader, James Ferguson.

How to Gain Influence in a New Administration

By Michael O'Bannon, Alex D. Tremble, Ryan Martin, and James Ferguson

Presidential transition is a nuanced process. To help navigate the process, it is important to understand the four major objectives associated with transitions:

1. Building a political team respected by the career service in order to manage the Executive Branch;
2. Establishing the incoming Administration's foreign and national security policies;
3. Establishing the incoming Administration's domestic policy agenda; and,
4. Transmitting a budget proposal to Congress that is focused on implementing presidential priorities.

Politically savvy leaders know that they must have a transition plan whether or not there is a change in the governing party. Whether the sitting President is replaced or is re-elected for a second term, there is always a transition of some sort following the election. One of the best sources of information regarding potential changes, and insights for how to demonstrate alignment of your interests with the interests of the incoming Administration, can be found in the candidate's campaign promises. These campaign promises will provide you with the critical information you need to build your transition plan.

Although U.S. Presidents are elected to a 4-year term, they have less time than that to fulfill their campaign promises. In the external environment of Twitter, Facebook, blogs, fake news, alternative facts, and 24-hour news cycles, in combination with midterm elections every 2 years that rightly, or wrongly, are seen as referendums on the President, time is at a premium. The internal environment is just as unrelenting in the demand to get things done as quickly as possible. The Federal Government is quite possibly the largest and most complex organization in the world with arcane rules meant to protect the public interest, but it also serves to slow the Administration's ability to get things done. Once the candidate is elected, he or she begins the recruitment and hiring process, which together with the learning curve monopolizes the first year of the term. After factoring in that the last year of the term is spent publicizing the Administration's accomplishments, that leaves years 2 and 3 to get things done, and the midterm election falls right in the middle of those years. By year 4, the President of the United States begins to lose influence as his term ends and people begin to focus their efforts on gaining favor with the next President.

Working with Political Appointees

There are around 4,000 Schedule C, presidentially appointed and Senate-confirmed positions in the Executive Branch. These employees are typically referred to as political appointees and have a substantial influence on the agencies they populate. Compared to career Federal employees, political appointee positions in the Federal Government are short term in nature, and political appointees can lose their jobs quite easily due to a number of reasons (e.g., nonperformance, the Administration losing its re-election campaign, or for purely political reasons). Thus, political appointees are under tremendous pressure to produce results quickly so that 1) substantial progress can be made on the President's agenda prior to the campaigning season and 2) the appointee has accomplishments to reference as he or she looks for the next job.

There is, however, a huge impediment to the ability of political appointees to accomplish the President's agenda, or their own private agenda. That impediment is what often seems to be inherent distrust between political appointees and career Federal employees. This distrust slows down the progress a political appointee can make, which only reinforces the distrust in this relationship. For the politically savvy and well-prepared leader, these pressures and challenges faced by the political appointee serve as opportunities.

Because we cannot adequately address everything about transitions within this chapter, we have decided to focus on two primary strategies for being successful through an Administration change: strategic planning and building trust.

Strategic Planning

In the months leading up to the election, the candidates will have already cemented their talking points and outlined their stances/priorities (e.g., their agendas). If you plan to approach this transition strategically, you must invest the time necessary to know and understand these talking points and how they relate to your agency, office, and/or program (your "interests"). If you choose not to invest the time necessary to understand how to demonstrate alignment of interests, you do so at your own risk. Although some Federal employees casually pay attention to politics as "entertainment" or to gain an idea of what candidates are planning for their agency, many do not find politics "important." The most successful Federal employees pay very close attention. Like experienced stock market investors, watching the market for clues on how to best position their next investment, politically savvy Federal leaders consume campaign information about each candidate to determine how they can demonstrate support for, and alignment of interests with, the winner's initiatives. Once you have a firm grasp of each candidate's agenda and voter base, you can begin the step 2.

Next, using the information you have collected, begin brainstorming programs/initiatives that support each candidate's positions. In most cases, this may entail tweaking an existing or old program with new messaging aligned with the messaging the candidates are using. However, once a candidate becomes President-Elect, you should quickly begin transitioning your ideas from conceptual to proposal phase. You must collect data on both pros and cons of your plan. Collecting information against your plan is essential and is a step that most do not take. Some practical guidelines follow:

1) It is more important to have a plan that will work than a plan that looks good. Knowing what might cause your proposals to fail will help you build a better program and have contingencies in place when things go wrong.

2) Understanding the potential downsides of your proposals will help you prepare for attacks because you can show you understand both sides of the issue, have thought through the possible negative externalities, and have created plans to address them should they occur.

3) You need to present the decision makers with the best information possible. If you hide information from them and things go wrong, they will not trust you in the future.

Having a good proposal is a start, but it is only a start. Once you have a good proposal, you must socialize the idea with key individuals. No one likes to be blindsided. Failure to socialize the idea, and to gain supporters in the process, can gain you unnecessary enemies—enemies who may block your plan simply because they were left out of the information loop. This is where having strong political skills comes into play. One who is politically savvy, as defined by the Office of Personnel Management, *identifies the internal and external politics that impact the work of the organization* and *perceives organizational and political reality and acts accordingly.* You have to know who needs to see this plan before a political appointee sees it. If you share it with the wrong individuals, they may try to undermine you for their own political gain or encourage you not to share your idea at all. The second scenario is much more likely, given that many people are afraid to interact with political appointees and would rather use the "wait and see" approach.

Once you have socialized your proposal and have received buy-in from key individuals within your organization, the idea can be shared with appropriate political executives. Again, this is a very politically sensitive process, and it is recommended that those who do not have a high degree of political savvy consult with a senior-level mentor or career coach who specializes in political strategy (https://www.linkedin.com/in/alextremble/). These situations can be difficult to navigate because you have to truly understand how your proposal impacts the rest of the agency. You would not want to suggest an idea that inadvertently negatively impacts another division and creates an entire office of enemies.

Remember, demonstrating apparent alignment of interests is so effective because the Federal bureaucracy is unwieldy at best, and for a new Administration with limited time to show success before beginning the next campaign, quick wins are lifelines.

Building Trust

Next, we discuss the art of building trust between you and the political executives in your agency. The first step to building trust with political appointees is to realize that they are people just like you. For some reason, people tend to view political appointees as omnipotent beings here for some nefarious purpose. In fact, this is generally far from reality. Political appointees, like you, are generally working at a particular agency because they truly care about its mission and how it impacts the public. In our many interactions with political appointees from various Administrations and parties, the political appointees cared about the mission just as much as the career employees did. But the political appointee may have different thoughts as to how the mission can and should be achieved. The largest difference we tend to see is related to the nature of the appointees' job—that is, they want results very quickly because of the time constraints discussed above.

Now that you see appointees as people, you should treat them like anyone else you are trying to build a relationship with—find commonalities. Appointees will typically have some sort of online presence and you should take the time to learn as much as possible about them. Once you have done your homework, you should ask them to go out for lunch, grab happy hour drinks, or see if they are willing to participate in a 30-minute informational interview. (You can find great tools for conducting informational interviews at https://www.youtube.com/AlexTremble.)

Given that these individuals are extremely busy, it can be difficult to schedule time with them, but do not give up. Once you have found an opportunity to connect with them, *do not* talk about work and *do not* ask them for favors. Everyone trying to meet them wants to discuss work and/or wants to ask them for a favor. Instead, focus your time on learning more about them: where they come from, what their interests are, how many siblings they have, and so on. Ultimately, your goal is to begin the trust-building process and to understand the appointees' goals and challenges. Once you understand their goals and challenges, you can begin finding ways to help them achieve their goals and overcome their challenges. This is not about you; this is about how you can help them be successful.

Two additional ways to build trust with new political appointees are by 1) identifying new opportunities for them to positively impact the agency and 2) helping them understand how to maneuver the internal politics of the organization.

First, having well-thought-out proposals that are aligned with the Administration's agenda is extremely helpful to appointees. This saves them valuable time, because they do not have to create and find career support for their own proposals when they arrive. It is important to not only design proposals that are aligned with the Administration's larger agenda, but to also propose new, more efficient ways to do business within the organization. If these ideas are successfully implemented, the appointees' trust in you will rapidly increase because you helped them achieve their goals. Secondly, you can more quickly build trust when you help them navigate the organization's internal politics. Again, time is extremely important to their success. If you can help them know whom to trust, whom they can depend on, and who the most influential employees are, then they will accomplish their goals faster and their trust in you will get stronger.

Finally, the old adage "it is lonely at the top" is 100% true. The higher you ascend within an organization, the less information you can share with others and the fewer people you can trust to be in your corner. But political appointees need someone they can trust and can be themselves around, someone they can bounce ideas off of. You should want to be that person. And, if you develop the skills and do the work necessary to gain the trust of political appointees, treat the relationship with the utmost care. If political appointees begin to suspect that you are acting in your own best interest or that you are sharing information that they told you in confidence, you will lose their trust, and you may find yourself in a lower position than when you started.

In closing, navigating the political minefield of a Federal agency is exciting and can have huge benefits for your career, but can also be detrimental to your career if you make a wrong move. Navigating organizational politics is never black and white. For example, if you successfully build a relationship with a political appointee, there will undoubtedly be those who will question your loyalty to the organizational mission and/or will view you as a "spy." These perceptions can and should be managed. For those with little or moderate experience working with political appointees, we recommend identifying a Senior Executive with strong political savvy to mentor you or finding a career coach who specializes in organizational politics.

Michael is the former Senior Executive Assistant and Controller to the Assistant Secretary for Fish and Wildlife Service and Parks at the U.S.

Department of the Interior (DOI). In addition to Michael's roles within DOI, he has served as an Examiner in the White House Office of Management and Budget, advised the DOI Secretary on budget issues, and served as an executive at the U.S. Export-Import Bank. Ryan joined the EOP Group, a management consulting firm, in 2006 as a program analyst and currently lobbies on behalf of various Fortune 500 companies in the energy, environmental, and chemical sectors. He is also a senior member of the EOP Foundation and its Federal training branch, EOP Education. His duties at the EOP Foundation include speechwriting, developing training courses for the public and private sectors, and cowriting EOP Foundation–authored studies, reports, and publications.

James Ferguson is an author and attorney. He has spent many years successfully leading teams and developing leaders of leaders in the public and private sectors. Alex Tremble is a career and leadership coach that helps Federal Government leaders further develop their political savvy, strategic networking skills, and leadership ability so that they are well positioned to excel in their current, or next, leadership opportunity. Subscribe to AlexTremble.com to learn more about the tools Alex offers his clients.

FEDERAL RESUME WRITING

T he truth is, at least dozens and perhaps hundreds of individuals will apply for the same Federal positions you apply for. In each case, a small team of human resources (HR) professionals (often a team of one) will review each resume to ensure that the applicant meets the minimum qualifications of the position. Only applications that survive this HR gauntlet will be referred to the position's hiring manager for further review. I once spoke with an HR professional who was responsible for reviewing 356 resumes submitted for one job opening. Additionally, each resume was between 10 and 12 pages long. That means that this one professional was responsible for reviewing over 3,560 pages of resumes for one job opening. Finally, this overworked HR professional must review all of the applications within a particular timeframe so that the hiring process can continue. That is for *one* vacancy announcement! Understandably, even the most conscientious HR professional, given the pressures of filling numerous vacancies and having limited time to do so, more often than not has little to no sympathy for resumes that are not perfect.

Hiring managers, too, are bombarded with hiring policies and "red tape," in addition to having to focus on the day-to-day operations of their offices. Most hiring managers know how important finding the right person is to the success of the organization's mission. But, because many managers do not hire very often and because there are *always* "emergencies" requiring their attention, they are rarely able to truly learn the hiring process and give it their full attention. Thus, individuals most likely to be interviewed are those whose applications immediately stand out and force the manager to recognize, almost instantaneously, that they could be "the One."

To stand out in the application process, the top priority is to submit an application so focused that the HR professional and hiring manager see you as the obvious choice. Although the Federal application process may seem daunting, the most successful Federal employees use strategies to increase the chances of their names being at the top of the list. To help identify some of these winning strategies, I reached out to Lily Whiteman, the author of *How to Land a Top-Paying Federal Job*, to share her expertise. I have known Lily for years. She is an extremely well respected career coach who also focuses on Federal employees.

Strategic Federal Resume Building Techniques for High-Performing Employees

by Lily Whiteman

How can you win over hiring managers and HR professionals? By submitting a fast-read, error-free, concise application that is targeted like a torpedo to each opening.

If you do, you are virtually guaranteed to vault ahead of most of your competition. Why? Because almost all applicants for Federal jobs submit long-winded, generic applications that draw about as much attention and excitement from hiring managers as your junk mail draws from you—and for many of the same reasons. I know this from my own experience as a hiring manager and from my interviews with 100⁺ other hiring managers.

Below I have listed the fundamental steps for creating a targeted, reader-friendly impressive application for Federal jobs:

- Instead of using the USAJOBS resume template, which generates hard-to-read resumes, upload your own well-formatted resume to USAJOBS. Most people take the simple approach of inserting their resume content into the USAJOBS template, but taking the extra step of uploading your own formatted version will increase your chances of standing out and being remembered.

- Identify qualifications required for your target job from the duties defined and qualification factors described in its vacancy announcement. This will ensure that your resume is strategically aligned with the position and that you are using the keywords that HR professionals need to see to assign you points.

- Include in your application a cover letter. Feature in your cover letter a table, with the left column on "your needs" and the right on "my credentials." Fill out the table by entering the top requirements for your target job in the "your needs" column and entering a concise summary of your best qualifications for each job requirement in the adjacent cell

66

in "my qualifications." More advice on creating such tables can be found in this blog entry:

https://www.govloop.com/community/blog/how-to-write-a-cover-letter/.

- Describe in your cover letter and resume only qualifications required by your target job—not qualifications you wish were required by your target job. Remember: No matter how many irrelevant credentials your application describes—impressive though they may be—they won't compensate for missing required credentials. For example, an application for a speechwriting job will probably fail if it omits or merely glosses over an applicant's experience writing speeches, but waxes on about his or her experience writing technical manuals and fact sheets.

- Format each job summary in your resume as a series of fast-read, achievement-oriented bullets. Each bullet should begin with an action verb, such as *produced, consolidated, increased,* and *advised.* (Google "resume action verbs" for more verbs.)

- Describe in each job summary in your resume specifics that match the substantive requirements of your target job. For example, if you were applying for a speechwriting job that will address environmental issues, your application should identify what environmental topics your speeches covered, who delivered your speeches, the audiences who heard your speeches, and the positive feedback drawn by your speeches.

- Describe "acting" positions in your application.

- Include headings in the job summary for your current job that correspond with the qualification factors in your target job's vacancy announcement. For example, if your target job's qualification factors include "leadership," "communication," and "strategic planning," use these terms as headings in your job summaries and group relevant bullets under each heading.

- Sequence bullets under each heading according to their relevance to your target job—not according to how much time you have devoted to the activities they describe. Likewise, provide the most details about your most relevant bullets, regardless of how much time you actually devoted to the activity they describe.

- Don't expect hiring managers to look for a needle in a haystack—they won't. Give hiring managers only the needle without the haystack. Scrupulously edit from your application credentials that won't help you land your target job—no matter how much they personally mean to you.

- Hyperlink your updated LinkedIn profile to relevant materials— including documents and multimedia products you produced and online praise of your work, such as reviews of presentations you delivered. Identify your LinkedIn address in a "Career Overview" or "Highlights" section of your hardcopy resume and state that it contains relevant hyperlinks.

- Grade yourself liberally on self-assessment short-answer questions in job applications; give yourself the highest rating for each of them that you possibly can without lying. For example, if you have solid credentials in a required subject area, rate yourself as an "expert."

Lily Whiteman is the author of How to Land a Top-Paying Federal Job. She is a career coach, writer, and speaker. Her website is http://www.IGotTheJob.net. This section was adapted from a https://www.govloop.com/community/blog/target-your-resume/ article with permission from Lily Whiteman.

ACHIEVING SUCCESS AS A YOUNGER LEADER

In my first role within the Federal Government, I was tasked with creating and managing the first Executive Leadership Development Program for a cabinet-level agency. Even as a 24-year-old millennial, I knew that I had to be extremely strategic and intentional to be taken seriously in this role. I mean, my customers were literally some of the highest-ranking officials within the Federal Government. I learned very quickly that to be successful in this role, I would need to do three things.

The first was to **build a strong reputation**. To build a reputation at this point in my career, I needed to be viewed as an expert in leadership development, while simultaneously not being perceived as a "know it all." To accomplish this, I scheduled formal and informal meetings with Senior Executive Service members on a regular basis to listen to their needs. During these meetings I would paraphrase what I heard to assure them that I fully understood their concerns. Following our meetings, I would use the information collected to develop programs specifically geared towards their needs. Yes, most of the leadership needs I gathered from the meetings were topics I already knew needed to be addressed. But it was the meeting process that was most important. Having the meeting with the executives allowed me one-on-one time to learn more about them and for them to learn more about me. I used those meetings as an opportunity to develop my reputation. In each meeting I was able to fully discuss leadership concepts and strategies with the executives (showing my expertise), while also asking a lot of questions about their requirements (which let them know that I was focused on their needs, not my own agenda).

Second, I focused on **listening and learning**. My supervisor at the time, and current mentor, had me accompany him to every executive-level meeting he could to expose me to the challenges executives dealt with on a daily basis. After each meeting, he and I would discuss both what people said and why they said what they said. I learned the back stories behind each position taken and the underlying reasons someone would disagree with another person when it did not seem to make sense. This allowed me to more quickly learn the organization's politics and improve my influencing skills. Since not all Federal employees have a mentor to teach them how to navigate office and organization politics, this navigation has become one of the focal points in my group mentoring programs. Understanding organizational politics is one of the key differences between those who excel in senior-level positions and those who do not.

Finally, I made sure I was **seen at the table**. One of my closest mentors told me early in my career that if I am always seen at the table, people will generally come to think that I belong there. This has definitely proven true for me. Because I found ways to attend more and more executive meetings and I was always in the executive corridor meeting with people, I began to be invited to more meetings and discussions having nothing to do with my portfolio. This was because people just expected me to take part in their conversations. This greatly increased my influence in the organization and also strengthened my reputation, which led to future job opportunities.

There are countless strategies younger Federal employees can use to be successful in their agencies. To highlight more of those strategies, I asked my colleague, Dr. Amina Gilyard James, to share some of her thoughts. Dr. James, the founder and principal consultant at Influence by AG, is a published writer and international speaker with 13+ years of experience working in Federal Government, higher education, and nonprofit organizations.

The Leadership Challenge:
Success Strategies for Black Millennials

by Amina Gilyard James, Ed.D.

An outstanding feature of most Federal Agencies in the United States is the vast diversity among their employees. With such diversity, it is the responsibility of the Agency to create environments where all types of employees have an equal opportunity to ascend to positions of leadership. Over the years, many advances have been made to promote conditions of equality within the workplace. However, the rise of a new cultural group—millennials—has unearthed new challenges to ensuring such fair treatment and opportunity. Unfortunately, millennials are often stereotyped as arrogant, unskillful, and naïve (Codrington, 2008). Stereotyping is dangerous in any circumstance, but it is especially so in the workplace because it can result in individuals being judged on the basis of their social identity group rather than their performance and potential (Roberson & Kulik, 2007). This is also troublesome given that being stereotyped negatively affects work-related outcomes, such as job attitudes, interpersonal negotiation, and the relationship between employees and their organization (Kalokerinos, von Hippel, & Zacher, 2014). Although developing the millennial generation into leaders may pose challenges for the Federal Government, millennials also face trials in terms of how to succeed in agencies that have not fully embraced or adapted to their presence.

Millennials in the Workplace
Who exactly are millennials? And why is their presence in the workspace such a big deal? The answer to both questions is anything but simple. Generally, millennials are considered those born between 1981 and 1996 (and thus 23 to 38 years old in 2019). One thing for certain is that the term *millennial* is more than a buzzword or the realization of commonly held perceptions. We've all heard them before—*"Oh, those millennials want so much so fast. The impatient generation!"* Sometimes I wish I could disappear when intergenerational conversations arise so that I am not grouped with *them* . . . the millennials.

Preconceived notions aside, there are markers of the millennial generation that distinguish it from other generations. In fact, we can look to generational theory to explain some of the differences that exist between generations. Generational theory is derived from sociological research dating back to the 1920s, and it attempts to explain how different generations develop different value systems and the impact those values have on their behaviors, attitudes, and interactions with the world (Codrington, 2008). As an overview, Strauss and Howe (2000) offered seven distinguishing traits of the millennial generation: special, sheltered, confident, team-oriented, achieving, pressured, and conventional. There is additional information available regarding characteristics of the millennial generation—much more than we have room to cover here.

Millennials are the second largest generation ever and as such is exceptionally diverse. For the remainder of this chapter, I will narrow the focus and discuss success strategies for a subset of the millennial generation—Black millennials. Historically, Black Americans have encountered significant barriers to attaining leadership positions within the Federal Government, partly as a result of institutionalized discrimination. For context, as of 2017, Black Americans accounted for 10.37% of senior executive service (SES) members (U.S. Office of Personnel Management, 2018). Research suggests that one challenge that Blacks continue to face is countering negative stereotypes. When we narrow the population even more and consider the experiences of Black millennials, it is likely they have to counter stereotypes associated with at least two social identity groups (i.e., Black and millennial).

The experiences of Black millennials, and other marginalized millennial groups, were not addressed by Strauss and Howe's broad generational theory. Consequently, their work has been criticized because of its lack of attention to matters of demographics and the social reality of race and ethnicity in American society (Wilson & Gerber, 2008). Subsequently, it is up to us as practitioners (and me as a Black millennial) to shed light on both the underlying organizational barriers for Black millennials aspiring to leadership within the Federal Government and the role of the individual in achieving that status. This chapter addresses the latter by providing strategies for Black millennials to be successful as they pursue leadership positions in their Agency.

Lead at All Levels

Before we go any further, let's clear up the myth that you can't be a leader unless you are in a *formal* leadership position within your organization. This is not true! In fact, the most influential leaders are often found at the so-called bottom in a traditional organizational hierarchy. Contemporary agencies that are keeping pace with global trends understand that leaders can exist anywhere in an organization. Millennials should use this current trend to their advantage and realize that now is the time to prepare themselves for leadership roles as the baby boomer generation exits the workforce in masses. Nonetheless, it is not at all easy for Black millennials to picture themselves as leaders. We have come a long way in regard to racial and ethnic diversity in the Federal Government; however, the number of Black employees in leadership, especially executive positions in the Government, is still conspicuously low in comparison to Whites. It can be discouraging to see such little representation of yourself in the highest executive positions. In fact, this lack of adequate representation in formal leadership can lead Black millennials to perceive that their upward mobility is limited. I offer this to Black millennials regarding their future in leadership: you add value and you will move up, so focus on preparing. First, your presence and contributions in meetings, workgroups, and as an advisor help your Agency tap into diverse knowledge and skills that will improve the Agency's operations and customer experiences. If you are not present, who is going to contribute your unique and valuable perspective?

Second, if you do not practice leading at all levels now, then you will not be ready when the opportunity arises for you to move into a formal leadership position. The key is to focus your practice on activities that will enhance your chances for advancement down the line. If you are unsure where to begin, and know you would like to advance to high-level leadership positions within the U.S. Government, you can begin honing your skills relative to the Office of Personnel Management's Executive Core Qualifications. These qualifications are typically used to determine a candidate's eligibility for entrance to the SES but are sometimes used more informally by organizations in the areas of performance goals and leadership development.

Executive Core Qualifications consist of the following five areas: leading change, leading people, being results driven, having business acumen, and building coalitions. Employees can find ways to enhance these qualifications in everyday work, as frequently or infrequently as desired. For example, try suggesting an improvement to office processes or procedures (leading change), serving as the lead on a working group (leading people), continuously developing your expertise and improving your customer service (being results driven), being an early adopter when the office begins using new technology or procedures and/or offering to help educate others (showing business acumen), and seizing every opportunity to reach out to or partner with internal and external entities to get the job done (building coalitions).

Define *Your* Professional

Black millennials have undoubtedly heard the gamut of cautionary tales from their parents, friends, and coworkers, all amounting to one old-as-time piece of advice: always remain professional. But what does being professional in the workplace *really* mean? For one, it should always include you being your authentic self. Most people misstep when trying to fit into a mold of what they think it means to be *professional* instead of being authentic. It may be tempting for Black millennials to attempt to fit a specific professional mold, especially if older, successful coworkers or mentors give them such advice. But, I challenge them to avoid conforming at all costs! While this may seem like a recipe for disaster in your Agency, it doesn't have to be. Learning how to tap into your identities as a resource can help you excel at work, but it is an art that is only learned with practice. Even further, when we look at the definition of professional or work identity, the difficulty of trying to separate your personal and professional identities becomes painfully obvious. Professional identity is defined as one's professional self-concept based on attributes, beliefs, values, motives, and experiences (Slay & Smith, 2011). One could argue from this definition that your identity in the workplace is, or should be, made up of the same elements as your personal identity. So instead of going against the grain and trying to adhere to a professional prototype, it works in your favor to be your authentic self, both in and out of the workplace. The only caution I give is to pay close attention to the culture of your organization for clues about which identity displays they deem inappropriate. If it seems from those clues that being your true self is not valued, I would consider changing Agencies before changing yourself.

Embrace the Teaching Moments

As with any new phenomenon in the workplace, there is an adjustment period—especially if you are in an Agency that does not prioritize diversity or change management. As a result, there will probably be instances in which Black millennials are exposed to marginalizing interactions. The situation can get more complex when you layer on power dynamics (e.g., a supervisor who says or does something inappropriate). It is easy to be insulted or taken aback by these types of interactions, and with good reason. The workplace should be a place where every individual is valued for his or her knowledge, skills, and abilities. But, there is plenty of anecdotal and scholarly research that tells us that this is not always the case. Consequently, we should prepare ourselves for the chance that we may encounter marginalizing interactions by considering how we want to manage them.

It is not my intention to minimize anyone's feelings, but to merely suggest reasons that one should consider embracing these types of interactions as teaching moments. Of course, the type of lesson that is taught should be at the discretion of the individual. First, an individual can play a key role in shifting the Agency's culture to be more inclusive by calling attention to inappropriate messages. Perhaps change won't happen right away, but if no one ever speaks up, then for sure the Agency's culture will remain the same. Second, by addressing these types of interactions head on, you are practicing your leadership skills. Being a leader is tough, and the stakes only get higher once you are in a formal leadership position. Having to navigate and resolve difficult interactions is a major part of leadership, and we only get better at it as we practice. Last, by countering marginalizing interactions, we can hopefully make things more supportive for other Black millennials who join the Agency.

Take Care of Yourself

Attending to our physical and mental health is probably the most important strategy for success. However, when we are in the midst of grinding in our careers, we can miss critical signals about the effect of work on our health. Negative work-related stressors can increase individuals' risk for depression, cardiovascular disease, and anxiety and decrease work productivity and efficiency. Additionally, individuals undergoing stress at work are vulnerable to experiencing burnout. Burnout is a phenomenon that results from chronic stress and is commonly associated with professionals who work in environments where they are constantly facing complex challenges—both work related and interpersonal.

The organization needs to play a central role in decreasing negative stress and the likelihood of employee burnout, but the responsibility of managing stress in a healthy way falls mainly on the individual. This is where self-care comes in. Self-care is an approach to living that incorporates behaviors that refresh you, replenish your personal motivation, help you grow as a person, and include intentional actions you take to care for your physical, mental, and emotional health. Every professional should commit to self-care, but it is especially important for professionals who are susceptible to increased levels of negative stress from being marginalized in the workplace—such as Black millennials. There is no one-size-fits-all approach to self-care; it is whatever works for you. For example, writing and traveling energize me, so as a self-care technique I journal occasionally so that my feelings are on paper instead of bottled up inside. I also plan regular small trips to step outside of my everyday element and enjoy a new space.

Conclusion

This brief chapter is meant to provide high-level strategies that Black millennial Federal employees can implement today with minimal risk in their current workplace. With the focus on civilian servant U.S. Government employees comes assumptions about the structure, culture, and processes of the organization. Therefore, this work does not intentionally take into account the challenges or advantages of Black millennials who work in nongovernment-sector organizations or professions. Also, the diversity among any group is too vast to capture in a few pages. Black millennials are no exception. Not only are Blacks and millennials not a monolith, but any one person can hold a multitude of identities that affect his or her existence in the workspace. I am hopeful, though, that this chapter will resonate with, and stimulate, Black millennials in all workspaces across identity dimensions.

References

Codrington, G. (2008). Detailed introduction to generational theory. *Tomorrow Today*. Retrieved from
http://www.tomorrowtodayglobal.com/2008/08/06/detailed-introduction-to-generational-theory/

Kalokerinos, E. K., von Hippel, C., & Zacher, H. (2014). Is stereotype threat a useful construct for organizational psychology research and practice? *Industrial and Organizational Psychology, 7,* 381–402. doi: 10.1111/iops.12167

Roberson, L., & Kulik, C. T. (2007). Stereotype threat at work. *Academy of Management Perspectives, 21*(2), 24-40.

Slay, H. S., & Smith, D. A. (2011). Professional identity construction: Using narrative to understand the negotiation of professional and stigmatized cultural identities. *Human Relations, 64*(1), 85-107. doi:10.1177/0018726710384290

Strauss, W., & Howe, N. (2000). *Millennials rising: The next great generation.* New York, NY: Vintage.

U.S. Office of Personnel Management. (2018). *Senior Executive Service report 2017.* Retrieved from https://www.opm.gov/policy-data-oversight/data-analysis-documentation/federal-employment-reports/reports-publications/ses-summary-2017.pdf

Wilson, M., & Gerber, L. E. (2008). How generational theory can improve teaching: Strategies for working with the "millennials." *Currents in Teaching and Learning, 1*(1), 29-44.

Amina Gilyard James, Ed.D., specializes in personal and professional development, strengths-based coaching, educational consulting, and organization development. She works with individuals and groups who want to optimize their talents and do so authentically. In addition, as a Certified Health Education Specialist (CHES), Dr. Amina incorporates aspects of wellness education into everything she does. She can be reached at agilyard@gmail.com or via her website at www.influencebyag.com.

THE COST OF REACHING YOUR GOALS

W hile most of this book focuses on the *planning* aspect of the GPS Success Method, this section is geared towards the *stamina* aspect. The reality is that if you want to play with the big dogs, you have to pay like the big dogs. Another popular way of saying this is that everything worth having comes at a cost. You may have the most clearly defined goals and the most strategic plans, but if you are not willing to pay the price, you are unlikely to be successful in reaching your goals.

So how, exactly, do you pay that price? Well, the price for reaching your goals must be paid for in four different currencies.

Energy

The first currency is energy. If you want more than others, you must be willing to work harder than others. Although hard work alone will not guarantee that you will reach your goals, hard work is critical to achieving success. And, the more success you desire, the longer you must be willing to work hard. To reach your goals, you must be comfortable working long nights and weekends if that is what it takes to produce the highest quality product that you can produce in a timely fashion. This does not mean that you should never have fun or never take time away from your goal, but it does mean that you will certainly have to make sacrifices to achieve your goals.

John C. Maxwell, a world renowned author, speaker, and pastor, shared that many people want to do what he does, but they do not want to do what he did. He spent years working tirelessly to get to the point he has gotten in his career. At one point he was publishing two books a year—which is no small feat. Was John crazy? I do not think so. I believe that he decided what he wanted in life and dedicated himself to reaching his goals. Now, because of his hard work, he is enjoying a life that he truly loves. Like John, I have worked many years, publishing articles, volunteering my time speaking at conferences, volunteering my coaching services, and studying my craft just so that I could get to where I am in life right now. I know that I will be working very hard for years to come, but I am comfortable with this knowledge because I know that I will accomplish the goals I set out to achieve.

Time

The second currency is time. Most people think that after defining their goals, they should be able to accomplish them in a few weeks or months. If that were true, everyone would be physically fit and financially secure. Unfortunately, that is not the case. But anything worth having is worth waiting for. The bigger the tree, the longer it takes for the roots to go down deep enough so that the tree can achieve majestic heights that inspire us for years to come. The bigger the goal is, the bigger investment of time you must be willing to make.

I like to share this thought with my clients: "You did not get to where you are today because of what you did today or even last week. You are where you are today because of what you did 10, 15, and 20 years ago. So why do you expect to reach a goal today that you just started working on 2 months ago?" To reach your highest goals, you must be willing to accept that you may be working towards them over many years. If you haven't started making progress toward your goals, now is the time. As one wise person said, "The best time to plant a tree was 20 years ago. The second-best time is today." Please do not be like most people who give up after a few months. Change takes time, and whenever you stop and start over again, you are only further delaying yourself from reaching your goals.

Emotion

The third currency is emotion. This is the currency that most people forget about, but it is critical. The truth is that when we invest our time and energy into a goal over long periods of time, we begin to become emotionally drained. We start to doubt ourselves. We begin to ask ourselves questions such as "Can I really do this?" "Am I doing it correctly?" and "Will this plan work?" If we are not strong emotionally, we may allow ourselves to give up before we have reached our goals. I spend a lot of time with my clients on developing and maintaining emotional fortitude. I teach my clients techniques to help them remain emotionally strong, stable, and present while they are working towards their goals.

Money

Finally, the last currency, and the currency that most people are reluctant to invest, is money. Do not get me wrong. People are more than happy to invest someone else's money into their development; they just do not want to invest their own money. For a long time, this described me as well. I was more than happy to turn down any development opportunity that I could not get my organization to pay for. Then I was invited to an event by some fairly influential people in Washington, DC. I asked, as I normally did, if I could attend at no cost and was told no. I asked my wife if I should attend and she told me that I would be crazy not to attend. Begrudgingly, I bought my ticket and a tuxedo for the event. By the time I returned from the event that night, my entire mindset on investing my money in my development had completely changed. I had met a number of very influential people who were going to mentor me, and I had been exposed to a completely different world. Since then, I have consistently invested in myself, whether it be buying books, attending training programs, or even securing my own executive career coach. Before my epiphany, I told myself that I "just did not have the money" for things like coaching or training. However, when I took a close look at my spending, I saw that there were many opportunities to spend my money better. Instead of eating out every night, my wife and I started cooking more; instead of going to bars, we would invite friends to the house; instead of buying Starbucks every day, we bought a home coffeemaker. People often do not realize that a part of professional development is developing better budgeting and spending practices. This is why I work with my clients on their budgets too.

At the end of the day, if you choose not to invest in yourself, you are choosing to keep countless doors closed. And, if you are one of the many employees who refuse to personally invest in training opportunities or mentoring programs that will help you reach your goals, you are literally putting your career and goals in the hands of your employer. Think about it. If you will only participate in training that your organization pays for, you are in effect giving your organization control over your development and your career.

Conclusion

Now that we have discussed these costs, I will share two very important points. First, to reach your goals, you must be willing to invest all four currencies. For example, if you choose to invest money, time, and emotion, but do not invest energy, you will not outperform your peers and competition. If you choose to invest your energy, money, and time, but not your emotions, you will begin doubting yourself and will give up once things get hard. Second, I promise you that reaching your goals will cost you more energy, time, emotion, and money than you plan for. Life will happen; something will go wrong, or you will be given an opportunity that you never thought you would have. Something will cause you to invest more than you plan, but I can also promise you that reaching your goals is worth it. I mean, this book cost me *much* more time, money, energy, and emotion than I had planned for. But, knowing that this finished product will help thousands directly, and millions indirectly, is 100% worth all that I have invested.

In short, if you invest all four of the above currencies towards reaching your goals, then you have true dedication. And, if you are truly dedicated to reaching your goals, you will not let anything stand in your way.

I have asked my good friend, James Ferguson, J.D., M.A., who we heard from in an earlier chapter, to continue this conversation on investing in one's self.

From GS to SES: Invest in Yourself

by James Ferguson, J.D., M.A.

The old man said to the stove, "Give me heat and I'll give you wood."
The stove said to the old man, "Give me wood and I'll give you heat."

This old fable is an appropriate allegory and a fundamental hurdle for most who yearn to make the journey from General Schedule (GS) to Senior Executive Service (SES) in the Federal sector or from employee to executive in the private sector. For the purposes of this discussion, the stove is your future, the wood is the knowledge you gain as you intentionally develop yourself, and the heat is the result that allows others to see you in the next-level job before you get the next-level opportunity. Many want the goal, whether it is GS-9, GS-14, or SES. Few are willing to pay the price to get there. Combine the allegory with the truism that an opportunity is only an opportunity if you are prepared for the opportunity, and the right choice for the old man, and for you if you want to become an SES, is clear. You must invest the time and resources to intentionally develop yourself in order to create the outcome you say that you want. The true measure of how much you want what you say you want is how much you are willing to pay the price to get it.

The secret of success in life is for a man to be ready for his time when it comes.
—Benjamin Disraeli

Many initially resist the idea that they must make a substantial investment of time and resources to reach the heights they say they want to reach. This is caused, in part, by the difference in the promotion criteria between lower-grade levels and higher-grade levels. At the lower-grade levels, you are often promoted automatically or because of increased technical skills, and the promotion scale is biased towards what you know instead of what you are. At each step up the organizational pyramid, the number of available positions decreases, the competition level increases, and progress requires increasingly higher levels of technical skills. In addition, as you get closer to the top of the pyramid, what was required at the lower level begins to matter less, until finally the promotion scale bias shifts from what you know to the multifaceted combination of skills, knowledge, experience, emotional and interpersonal intelligence, thought processes, and behaviors that comprise what you are in the work space.

The early promotions can be misleading because they don't prepare you for the shift that higher levels of promotions require. So, while the early promotions may feel good, they can result in a false set of expectations regarding what is required to get yourself promoted at the higher levels and may lead you to overlook the importance and process of developing yourself, not just improving your technical skills, in order to achieve your highest goals.

Invest in Yourself

There are literally thousands of very good books and courses in the personal development genre, but none of them will make an appreciable difference in your life if you do not believe in the importance and ultimate benefits that you will derive from a commitment to developing yourself. Your belief system fuels your desires and drives what you do, what you think about what you do, and how you feel about what you do. If you don't believe in the importance of personal development, you are unlikely to make the commitment to undertake the effort required to go from GS to SES.

Even if you don't believe in personal development, all is not lost. It is easier to act your way into feeling than it is to feel your way into acting. With that in mind, commit to 20 minutes of personal development each day. I recommend that you begin with studying the importance of personal development.

Assess Your Environment

An often overlooked step along the path from GS to SES is the importance of creating an environment around you that is conducive to achieving the success you say you want to achieve. A poor environment for personal development has the same effect as an open window when you are trying to heat a room while a polar vortex is raging outside. The room might get warmer, but a lot of the heat will be wasted as it goes out the window. Even less heat in a proper environment where the window is closed will likely result in a warmer room. The same is true for your personal development. In the right environment, the positive results emanating from your personal development efforts will come to the fore much more rapidly than they will in a poor environment.

When establishing the right environment to maximize your personal development efforts, a fundamental requirement is to be intentional about how you spend your time and who you spend your time with. Be intentional about surrounding yourself with people who are wiser than you, smarter than you, and know more about the topic than you do—people who have already traveled the road you want to travel and who are willing to share their knowledge and experience with you. Be intentional about finding people who can and are willing to invest in you by giving honest helpful insight on your personal development needs. When possible, talk to these mentors and coaches directly. Beyond that, be intentional about getting in the room when they speak, reading their books, listening to their speeches and interviews, watching their videos, and going to their trainings.

Cherish Your Time

Be intentional about avoiding people who belittle your dreams, discourage your efforts, and spend more time complaining about their circumstances than changing their circumstances. With everything you see hear and spend your time on, ask yourself: Am I investing my time or wasting my time? Is this helping or hindering my journey? Answering those questions may or may not stop you from binge watching reruns, but they may give you a standard for examining your behaviors and help you think about the conscious and subconscious choices you make and how they impact your ability to achieve your goals.

Learn to Listen

To build an environment conducive to developing yourself, take the advice of former Central Intelligence Agency Director and Secretary of Defense Robert M. Gates. In his book *A Passion for Leadership*, he said "never miss a good chance to shut up." It is difficult to listen, learn, and talk at the same time. Even if you are wise enough to surround yourself with people who know more than you and are willing to invest their time in you, you will not maximize learning unless you are listening more than you are talking. Since most of us were born with two ears and one mouth, it seems reasonable to assume we can listen more and talk less.

Take Ownership

Lastly, but arguably most importantly, take ownership of your personal development. Taking ownership requires you to let go of all aspects of victimhood. Don't blame people, don't blame circumstances, and don't make excuses for where you are in your life personally or professionally. Letting go of victimhood puts all the power you need back in your hands. You have the power to create the life you want. Because you are the creator, you can change everything that you create. Just as a stone sends ripples whether it lands in a pond, a puddle, or an ocean, as you change the world around you will change. Take whatever action you need to take to build a better you, to build a better life, and to make your contribution towards building a better world. Honestly assess where you are considering where you want to go, develop a plan to change whatever needs to be changed, and get moving on the path from GS to SES.

James Ferguson, J.D., M.A., is an author and attorney. He has spent many years successfully leading teams and developing leaders of leaders in the public and private sectors. Those interested in reaching out to James can reach him at godspraise@hotmail.com.

OVERCOMING DISCRIMINATION

Now this is not the end. It is not even the beginning of the end.
But it is, perhaps, the end of the beginning. —*Sir Winston Churchill*

My wish for you is that this book represents the end of the beginning of your latest step towards achieving your goals. I encourage you to read this book and reread this book, highlighting passages that resonate with you or raise questions for you. Continue doing this until the treasure trove of information in the book becomes a part of you and pushes you forward on your journey to success.

My mentoring and public speaking events have provided me with opportunities to hear and learn from Federal employees all around the United States. So, as uncomfortable as it may be to discuss, I think it is important that I acknowledge and address some unfortunate events that you will undoubtedly face on your journey to success. As I travel across the country speaking to different groups about reaching their career goals, I am usually asked some form of the following question: "Have you ever encountered discrimination in the workplace and how did you deal with it?"

My answer is always the same, although not everyone agrees with my perspective. Yes, I have experienced discrimination at various times during my career. But so what? Discrimination is silly, shortsighted, wastes talent, does a disservice to the organization, and reflects poorly on the person responsible for the discriminatory behavior. I obviously do not like being discriminated against, but the reality is that there are only two ways to deal with it. You can allow someone else's conscious or unconscious ignorance to stop you from reaching your goals, or you can recognize that their actions are just another obstacle that you have the skills to overcome on your way to the top. I obviously chose the latter approach. In fact, my exact response to people who ask me this question is that I refuse to allow anything or anyone to come between me and my goals.

On your way to career success, I can assure you that something will go wrong and you will be treated unfairly, whether it's because of the color of your skin, the state or country you are from, your level of formal education, or your accent, financial status, sex, or a host of other qualities that make you unique. You have to ask yourself this question: Am I going to let this situation tear me down, or is this situation an opportunity to make me stronger? When I discuss this topic, I am always reminded of one of my favorite Ted Talks by a man named Joseph Logan (2014). During his talk, he made the case that there is no "silver lining" in the crisis that we face. He shared that crises are generally terrible events that are painful, uncomfortable, and emotionally, cognitively, and financially draining. There is no inherent good in crisis, but there are opportunities—opportunities to grow stronger, smarter, and more resilient. That is why I genuinely become excited every time I am put in an uncomfortable situation (see Tremble, 2019 for more on this topic.)

The Federal Government sorely suffers from a lack of diversity within its senior leadership ranks. The question is not if this will change, but if you have prepared yourself to take advantage of the inevitable change that is quickly approaching. I encourage you to prepare yourself by studying this book, developing the skills that my coauthors and I have identified, sharing what you have learned with others, and committing yourself to paying the cost to achieve your dreams.

In closing, the best advice I can give you on this topic is to take the following two steps. First, accept that the world is not a perfect place and that you *will* be treated unfairly at some point. Second, refuse to let that stop you from reaching your goals. If necessary, fight for your dreams or find another organization, but refuse to let anyone control your destiny or stand in the way of your bright future.

To dive deeper into this topic, I have asked one of my mentors, Tarrazzia Martin, to share her journey from GS-2 to the Senior Executive Service. Tarrazzia is not only one of the most impressive women I know, as you will see from her chapter, but she is also my aunt.

References

Logan, T. (2014). *The upside of crisis* [Ted Talk]. Retrieved from https://www.youtube.com/watch?v=rVtMYpOSNmA&t=381s

Tremble, A. (2019). *The Federal career coach: Why I now get excited every time something goes wrong* [Video]. Retrieved from https://www.youtube.com/watch?v=ky5lYeiSj58&t=279s

Tarrazzia's Journey:
One Woman's Rise from the Mailroom to the Boardroom

by Tarrazzia Martin

I grew up in a small town in Utah called Ogden. I was raised in a middle-class multicultural family of business owners and pioneers who set the bar to achieve your dreams through hard work, determination, and a strong spiritual and moral posture. Becoming a public servant was an aspiration. As I started my Federal career after completing college, it was apparent that the journey would be a long and serpentine road to achieve my initial career goal of becoming an influencer as a senior executive in the Government—within a 10-year period.

As one of my favorite motivational speakers, Les Brown, said, "I was *hungry*" and knew I would make an impact on the world. I did not know what that impact would be, but I knew I was destined to do something great. I felt that my college experience at Utah State University, my drive, my talents, and my determination to make an impact on the world would catapult me into a prosperous and noteworthy career.

Internal Revenue Service in Utah

I started my career as a GS-2 at the Internal Revenue Service (IRS) Service Center in Utah. I started off literally in the mailroom working the night shift. The team included a mix of newbies or college graduates starting their careers as public servants, middle-tier staff who had been there for about 10 years, and experienced Elders who had been there for well over 10 years. The environment required very little brain power, but we had fun, learned how to work as a team, and created positive friendships and social relationships. After about 3 months in the mailroom, I was elevated to a GS-3 and then reassigned to the operations processing area. This horizontal move allowed me to obtain recognition from leadership, learn more, and make more money.

Being a woman of color working in Utah brought challenges. The covert racism at the service center was real but also hard to detect. The people in Utah are genuinely nice. At that time the population in Utah was about 1% minority and 99% white. I would say 99% of the employees at the IRS Service

Center were Mormon/Latter-Day Saints. I felt love from many of them, but I felt subtle racism from many others. During my short time at the service center, I experienced one extreme racial incident from a coworker who thought I was promoted too soon. The issue resolved itself because I was reassigned to a new area to avoid any further conflicts. It seemed to be a win-win for both parties at the time.

At the end of the day, my biased coworker was never reprimanded for his actions or racial bias, and it seemed I was rewarded for not making an issue of the incident. I was subsequently given the opportunity to move up and out, and I did just that.

I held various positions within the IRS Service Center but eventually took a new position in Salt Lake City to work for the IRS Legal Appeals Office. This assignment was a promotion and a more challenging role. Being in a law office, learning the ropes in the legal process, and understanding and appreciating what legal professionals do was a perfect learning environment. I respected and befriended the attorneys, and they mentored me. At one point, I thought about becoming an attorney and changing the world through legal means, but I learned quickly that my journey would lead me elsewhere. Did I mention that I was *hungry?*

My supervisor for my new position was the office manager, a middle-aged white man who had lived his whole life in Utah. He held a narrow view of women and an even narrower and naïve view of people of color. He automatically saw me as less than, a villain and a threat. He was looking for a docile and demure white administrative assistant who would simply do what she was told. I did not fit the bill.

He would provide job expectations for me and smile and behave cordially; however, under that smile was a vicious condescending terrorist. He began to undermine everything I did, on a mission to make my life miserable. My work was never good enough; my presence was never welcomed. It felt like I was in a slave plantation owner relationship. I was good enough to be inside the office as an administrative worker, but I was to remember my place.

I felt undervalued every day working in the office. The saving grace for me was the attorneys that I worked with, who took the time to teach me how to write with legal persuasion, how to understand and apply negotiation techniques, and how to proofread legal documents—skills I still use today. These attorneys were diverse; many were from other states and backgrounds and had experience working in different offices around the country. They saw my value and encouraged and rewarded me by providing feedback on my daily tasks and assignments. They often apologized for the office manager's behavior and tried to shield me from his attacks; however, at the end of the day, the office manager was the plantation owner, and he dictated the work of all the staff and decided who was rewarded or reprimanded.

Then the dreaded performance evaluation process began. As expected, he developed an unfair performance evaluation for me with very harsh words. It was a blatant attack on me as a person and my abilities. He gave this rating in spite of feedback from the attorneys, who indicated that I performed well and required some progressive improvements in clerical tasks but overall should receive an excellent rating. I was infuriated. I decided to fight the evaluation on the basis of Affirmative Action/Equal Employment Opportunity (EEO) rules. I fought a very good fight with lots of documentation to justify my perspective. I ended up winning the case, and the resulting decision was that I would be transferred to another office to avoid further conflict.

I began to see the pattern. *At the end of the day, the office manager was never reprimanded for his actions or racial bias, but I was given the opportunity to move up and out, and I did just that.*

With goals driving my every move, I was well on my way to my next position. I had three different positions within 2 years, with each one paying more than the last. I believed I was in a good place. In spite of the office manager's opinion, I had built enough equity in people outside the office and with attorneys in the office to leave with a positive record and one that earned me my next position. I was driven, my ego was on high, and I felt I was well respected and positioned for making an impact.

Internal Revenue Service in Washington, D.C.

I began applying for jobs in Washington, D.C. It didn't matter what Agency or Bureau; I just wanted to be in Washington, D.C., the hub of the Federal Government, and to be in the Nation's Capital. After applying for over 40 positions and after several months of waiting for a response, I was selected for two positions at the same time—one with the IRS and one with the Commerce Department. I took the IRS position. I had been in Utah my whole life. I spent summers in Los Angeles, Denver, and Las Vegas, but had little experience with the East Coast. This was a bold, brazen move, and I did it with pure confidence!

So it began—my journey in Washington as a GS-5 at the IRS offices on Pennsylvania Avenue. It was a new level and a new world for me. After several years and many mentors, I finally figured out how to be successful as a GS employee in Washington. It required being good at your job and being able to effectively communicate and collaborate with the leadership team above you and your peers to get the job done. I soared to the next levels and made great acquaintances along the way. I had mentors along- side me, above me and working for me... I learned that everyone can teach you something, you just must be willing to listen. These mentors helped me to understand and navigate both the office and Washington politics. Both of which can be detrimental to your career if not managed wisely.

As I moved up in ranks, I learned the importance of growing your network and your skills. I decided to always seek to expand my horizons. Remember, I was hungry!

My initial job in Washington was as a program analyst in the IRS Chief Information Officer (CIO) Office, where I was assigned to work on the IRS Modernization Project. My duties were to create simulation models for the IRS tax business processes and to document these simulated processes into technology software while identifying automation opportunities. My superiors believed in me and empowered me to learn everything technology. I soon became a critical asset on the team and was promoted to the GS-7 level within a year. As I served in various team lead and project management roles, within 4 years, I was promoted to a GS-11.

As a team leader with the IRS Modernization Program, I was asked to participate in a project to enhance the IRS mainframe and database to support health care providers in tracking health benefits for U.S. citizens. I was asked to work alongside several rising IRS superstars to make the project a reality. This is when the racial bias reared its ugly head. I was on a team of senior IRS professionals that felt I was either too young, too immature, or not skilled enough to add value to this important White

House–directed project. The competitive nature of the Federal GS scale is worth mentioning here. As you rise further up the ladder in the organization, the opportunities to get promoted become very narrow in terms of leadership positions. There are only so many GS-14s and GS-15s available in each organization, and each GS-11 and GS-12 is vying for the next GS-13 position. So when you are working on a project that is an organizational priority and allows you to show your talents, you begin to see competitive war games at play. During this period, I learned about the life-changing book by Robert Green entitled *The 48 Laws of Power.* I encourage all of my mentees to read this book to master the art of politics.

One person during this period actually called me a racial slur in one of our meetings. I ignored it but did not forget. I held on to the issue for over 8 months and then finally brought it to management's attention. After project completion, the team won big accolades from the White House. Hillary Clinton led this initiative and gave the team and the IRS major praise for our work on the project. I was then reassigned to a new office because of team and office jealousy and blatant discriminatory acts. Leadership valued me and decided to provide a new opportunity for me to avoid any further conflict. Sound familiar? I didn't challenge this reassignment because I was hungry!

At the end of the day, the coworker was never reprimanded for his actions or racial bias, but I was given the opportunity to move up and out, and I did just that.

Department of Treasury and General Services Administration
I took the opportunity to work on a new project at the Department of Treasury, the IRS's parent organization. The role was project manager for a department-wide telecommunication program. We were so successful and created such positive change with the program that I was promoted within 9 months to a GS-13. The project allowed me to grow professionally and personally as a leader. This assignment turned out to be the best chess move I could make. I was able to affect technology and contracting improvements to support effective and efficient telecommunication services for the IRS and the other 13 bureaus.

As I worked within Treasury, I was promoted to a GS-15 within 2 years and then volunteered to be reassigned to the General Services Administration (GSA) to lead the acquisition team on the FirstGov.gov project, now called USA.gov, the largest and most recognized Government content management and search engine resource. Oh yeah, I was definitely *hungry*!

Working at GSA was an awesome experience; we were at the hub of the creation of a program called Citizen Services. This program transformed Government's view of how to focus on the citizens' needs and to ensure Federal, State, and Local Government data and information resources were aligned with the needs of the citizens. My role was to create the strategy and acquisition plans to create a real-time content management solution leveraging various technologies to meet this unprecedented Government-wide requirement. We were very successful! The White House praised our team, and we won countless awards and recognitions. It was a blast introducing new technology and innovation to the Government ranks as part of a program called Electronic Government.

After a couple of years, I ended up leaving GSA primarily due to a sexual harassment scandal between one of our leaders and a paid consultant. I was neither the victim nor the perpetrator but an innocent bystander who became the fall guy for being a whistleblower. I was encouraged to make a change to avoid further conflict with the persons involved.

At the end of the day, the victim and perpetrator were not admonished for their actions on the job. Both parties moved on and up the ladder, while the bystanders were admonished for being in the wrong place at the wrong time. I was given the opportunity to move up and out, and I did just that.

Department of Homeland Security

After my successful time at GSA, I was requested to work at the newly formed Department of Homeland Security (DHS). DHS was created from merging 22 Federal Agencies and bureaus to protect the homeland from domestic and foreign terrorism. I served as the Deputy Director for Telecommunications and Infrastructure services. This was right after the 9/11 terrorist attacks. We were determined to make the new DHS a force to be reckoned with.

My star had risen quickly at GSA, but within DHS I was considered the golden child. I rallied resources together and made things happen. In mobilizing a new Federal entity, we were aligning infrastructure, applications, data centers, and business processes to collaborate against terrorism. It was a really tough job, but because I was so successful at managing the telecommunications and infrastructure programs, after less than a year, I was elevated yet again to become the first CIO for the U.S. Citizenship and Immigration Services (USCIS), a bureau under DHS. Although I was a GS-15 at the time, I was assured my SES status as part of this new role. Our new post-9/11 mission was to create technologies to identify and track suspected or known terrorists who may have entered the U.S. under the pretense of immigration or travel visas.

The USCIS's culture was very closed against outsiders and outsider opinions. USCIS did not ask for a CIO, nor did they think they needed one. I was very honored for the opportunity to serve as the CIO, but the environment was toxic. This is when the big moment occurred: I was promoted to a term appointment SES position as the CIO for USCIS. I thought I had finally arrived. I was so wrong! I walked right into a political warzone fraught with racism and discrimination.

I served in this position with fervor and passion. In fact, I feel that I learned to be a leader while in this position. Yes, it was a tough job, but I had been given the opportunity to create a new organization from the ground up. By the time I was finished, I had over 300 employees and contractors working for me and making huge inroads to overhaul the technologies of immigration in our country.

I filed an EEO lawsuit against the leaders of the USCIS for discrimination and harassment, based on a hostile work environment created by the management team. In one specific incident, I was called a nigger by a senior leader (it was under his breath but he clearly used the N word). This incident was my wake-up call. I knew the circumstances were dire for me and I could be injured by the anger these people felt. I yielded a lot of power as the CIO. I managed resources and made decisions that those holding on to the status quo were afraid of. I was a threat. After months of abuse, disrespect, torment, racial undertones and overt racial slurs, and the pending lawsuit, I decided it was time to move forward to my next challenge.

At the end of the day, the leadership team within USCIS was never reprimanded for creating a hostile work environment or for their racial bias. Again, I was given the opportunity to move up and out, and I did just that.

The Intelligence Community

My determination to find my next opportunity led me to a new position within the intelligence community leading a program to improve information sharing between Federal law enforcement and intelligence agencies. It was an important job and I was personally requested to take on this role because of my experience with USCIS and Treasury.

I was promoted within 3 months as a senior intelligence executive (which is unheard of in that culture—many people work 10 to 20 years to earn an executive position within the intelligence community). It made me a target. I was a woman of color, an outsider, and a favorite child to the leadership team. My light was too bright. During my tenure within an unnamed intelligence agency, I served in various leadership roles for about 8 years. During that time, I filed one EEO complaint for job and pay discrimination and won that case after years of negotiations.

With one small voice fighting a behemoth organization, it was very intimidating. I stuck it out and endured the pain and torment of the battle. As you can imagine, if I tell you any more about it, I could be shot . . . lol, just kidding. No, really, I could be shot!

In Conclusion

My journey from the mailroom at the IRS Service Center in Ogden, Utah, to an agency within the intelligence Community in Washington, D.C., has been enlightening and gratifying. Although I have filed several lawsuits against the Government for unfair, racial, and hostile work environments, I would not change one thing about my journey. Because of my personal drive, I was able to move up and out of organizations to my benefit. As an individual, my career has been very successful for a woman of color from Utah. I was driven and very hungry!

I fought a good fight and won many of my battles along the way. It was challenging, and there were days when I felt I could not continue. Each challenge brought life lessons that made me a bit stronger. My grandmother used to always say: "Know your worth." My worth was not tied to obtaining the Senior Executive Service position or to what my job title or bank account say. My personal value and worth come from within. It took me many years to learn that it doesn't matter what people think; just do your best and be your best in spite of the circumstances around you.

After the first two racial or bias-based incidents, I learned these were patterns of behavior seen often in Government. We usually don't deal with the real issue of institutional racism. We all know it exists, but we simply sweep issues under the rug and make everyone feel good without addressing the root cause and the systemic issues within a sick organization. When you couple an individual's racial bias with an organization's dysfunctional cultural norms of racial and discriminatory behaviors, the combination can be lethal.

In most Federal agencies, the organizational norm for incidents of inequity is to remove the person from the environment. This decision can cause long-term negative effects for both the individual and the organization. Overt and covert racism and sexism are causing divisiveness among the ranks of our Government. The question is: What can we do about it?

At the end of the day, all organizations have a responsibility to address institutional bias and racism and to reprimand individuals who exhibit it. We must hold everyone at all levels accountable for their acts of racial bias. The Federal policies and guidelines exist and are written to protect individuals from these behaviors. However, organizational leaders do not follow these policies, and the risks for not complying are minimal. When the policies are followed, organizations find ways to manipulate the intent and meanings of these policies to suit their specific political need and desired outcome.

The Federal workforce is changing and becoming more diverse—not only in ethnic background, religion, and culture, but in ideas. The new Federal workforce diversity model is what will sustain us as a strong and cohesive workforce for centuries to come. We must embrace each other's differences and accept new ideas while we embrace innovation. This new model will create nationwide strength and solidarity across our Government and improve our global posture as a Nation.

Each individual must make it a personal goal to address this challenge through assimilation of new ideas and by keeping an open mind and heart to hear and understand others to achieve organizational greatness. As a favorite author of mine, Stephen Covey, said, "First seek to understand." When we do that, we can reduce racism and any bias we may hold. Each of us must encourage all Federal employees and leaders to shed the old operating models and broken thought processes. Each of us must open our minds to systematically work together to dismantle separation tactics and divisiveness wherever we see it. If we disenfranchise one of us, we violate all of us. Our differences make us stronger when we embrace each other as part of this vast universe.

Don't be a bystander. Be an activist. For our Government to survive and remain effective for the people, we must represent the people we serve. We must all contribute toward creation of a unified Government *vision*. The goal of this vision is to hold each other accountable to do our part to enable fairness and equity to all individuals and to work in unison to become a prosperous and successful dominating force.

Ms. Tarrazzia Martin is a powerhouse change maker, named the "Government Transformation Queen" by *Federal Computer Week*. She is a senior executive and entrepreneur with over 25 years of leadership and technology experience across multiple market sectors. She is an expert in Government practices, including the areas of digital strategies, strategic planning, information technology, security operations, public policy, portfolio and performance management, acquisition planning, and program/project management. Tarrazzia is owner of a private policing and surveillance agency, CEO of an IT consulting firm, and owner of a nonprofit that serves disadvantaged communities in the Washington, DC, area. A voice of the people, Tarrazzia is often asked to share her perspectives as a rising Federal employee who moved from the mailroom to the board room. Her lighthearted approach to life and her serious message attract audiences from academic, Federal, State, local, and commercial markets. You can contact her at Tarrazzia.Martin@yahoo.com.

IN CLOSING

N ow that you have reached the end of this book, and (hopefully) picked up some valuable growth strategies you can start applying, you may have noticed there was no section about something that the vast majority of government employees rely on. Something they believe will magically bring them the success they always dream of – and that's "hard-work".

Now you may be thinking: "But Alex, why don't you 'preach' hard-work? Won't my boss be impressed if I put in long hours? Doesn't hard-work increase my chances of getting promoted to that leadership position I seek?"

Well, although many coaches may have you believe hard-work is all it takes, it's really not. If you still lack the ability to maneuver in political environments, and influence how others perceive you - even pushing yourself to work for hours on end will not get you very far in the government workplace. Think about it this way, as of this book there are over 2 million employees employed by the Federal Government. If even half of those people are "hard-workers" you are now competing with over 1 million individuals for a limited number of senior level positions.

And as a result, all your efforts will become just another burden to bear – another blockage to your career success.

So does hard-work pay off? Yes. Is it a requirement for success? Absolutely. But does it mean that every employee who "puts in the hours" will become a high achiever in the government world? Definitely not.

Like I mentioned in the beginning of this book, one of the keys to success is realizing there is no need to rebuild the wheel every time. No matter what you do, there are always people who have gone through the same process, succeeded, and now know which strategies work, and which don't. Just think: every time you look at a successful person, whether it's a professional athlete, actor, or a government leader, there is always someone standing behind their success – a coach, or a mentor.

To put it simply, there is no reason to shy away from asking for advice.

Having someone who is personally invested in your success, keeps you grounded, and ensures you make the right decision every step of your career journey is priceless. Not to mention it will noticeably accelerate your learning curve and help you avoid embarrassing mistakes and frustrations that plague most government employees.

And that's exactly what my GPS Success Strategies Newsletter (www.AlexTremble.com) is here for. As soon as you subscribe, not only will you gain free access to my career success strategies, but you will also learn more about my Group Career Mentoring Programs which are uniquely designed to teach you how to 1) successfully navigate organizational politics, 2) build strong and influential networks, 3) develop a reputation that makes you stand out from the crowed, and 4) identify the skills and experiences necessary get you to the next level.

This book is just the tip of the iceberg of what it really takes to reach those highly coveted leadership positions. My newsletter, mentoring programs, and courses are here to help you build upon the foundations you've learned in this book, and guide you every step of your journey to that career success.

Finally, if you're a training manager or a supervisor reading this book, here's one more thing you should take back to your organization: Don't just rely on sending your employees to one-off trainings and having them learn about team building, team leading, conflict management etc, hoping they will get promoted. If they have no idea how to politically maneuver and influence others, no amount of leadership skills will make them successful.

It's like teaching someone which directions a chess piece can move without teaching them any chess strategy. Can they play chess? Yes. But their chances of winning? Slim to none.

If you want to get your workers "out of the rut" and position them for success, sign up for my newsletter and mentoring programs at AlexTremble.com and arm your employees with the savviest political career strategies!

ACKNOWLEDGMENTS

I would like to thank my amazing wife, Su Hlaing Win Nu, for being so patient with me while I locked myself in the study at home every night for four straight months to finish this book. I also thank her for not only giving her unwavering love, but for holding me accountable for reaching her high expectations of me. I thank all of my coauthors for their commitment and for dedicating themselves to producing such powerful content. I thank my mentors (Jerry Gidner, Gail Adams, Rene Redwood, Joe Ward, George McDonald, Tara Morrison, and Tarrazzia Martin), friends (Brennan Richardson, Dominique Broadway, Andrew Lee, Kirin Kennedy, Douglass and Janice Garland, Waverly Gordon, Vernon Robinson, Q. B. Driskell, Hla Hla Win, and many many more), my mother and father (Robin and Johnny Davis), my in-laws (Hnin Yi Aye and Maung Maung Myint), and all of my brothers, sisters, and cousins for the encouragement they have given me over the years. I thank the political appointees who allowed me to interview them off the record (you know who you are). Finally, I thank you, reader, for taking the time to read this book. You mean a lot to me and I hope that you reach the success of your dreams!

ABOUT THE EDITOR

Alex D. Tremble is an author, businessman, and a John C. Maxwell Certified Speaker and Coach. With over 10 years' experience in overseeing executive leadership development programs, senior leadership mentoring programs, and career coaching, he is the founder and CEO of the leadership development company GPS Leadership Solutions.

Alex's first book, *The GPS Guide to Success*, focuses on helping people identify their goals and create strategic plans to reach them. He has written numerous articles on leadership development and career progression and was a contributing author in the *ATD Talent Management Handbook*.

When Alex is not traveling around the country speaking on navigating organizational politics, career advancement, and influencing strategies, he and his wife volunteer to support youth and the homeless population. He also enjoys international travel and escaping civilization for a nice hike in the woods; he once trekked 12 miles through the Grand Canyon. As far as the future is concerned, Alex simply hopes that he will one day positively impact the lives of millions of people around the world.

Alex has a B.A. in Psychology and Sociology from William Penn University and an M.S. in Industrial and Organizational Psychology from the University of Baltimore.

You can contact or follow Alex D. Tremble at
https://www.facebook.com/FederalCareerCoach/
https://www.linkedin.com/in/alextremble/

https://instagram.com/alexdtremble
https://www.youtube.com/alextremble

Made in the USA
Middletown, DE
26 August 2019